The Rise of Humans: Great Scientific Debates

John Hawks, Ph.D.

PUBLISHED BY:

THE GREAT COURSES
Corporate Headquarters
4840 Westfields Boulevard, Suite 500
Chantilly, Virginia 20151-2299
Phone: 1-800-832-2412
Fax: 703-378-3819
www.thegreatcourses.com

Copyright © The Teaching Company, 2011

Printed in the United States of America

This book is in copyright. All rights reserved.

Without limiting the rights under copyright reserved above,
no part of this publication may be reproduced, stored in
or introduced into a retrieval system, or transmitted,
in any form, or by any means
(electronic, mechanical, photocopying, recording, or otherwise),
without the prior written permission of
The Teaching Company.

John Hawks, Ph.D.
Associate Professor of Anthropology
University of Wisconsin–Madison

Professor John Hawks was born and raised in Norton, Kansas. In his youth, he followed science but did not seem destined for a career in it. At Kansas State University, he studied English and French literature, earning a B.A. But a chance to teach bone labs inspired him to follow through with a dual degree in Anthropology. Making the switch to science, he went on to earn his M.S. and Ph.D. in Anthropology at the University of Michigan, specializing in paleoanthropology.

After a postdoctoral fellowship at the University of Utah specializing in human genetics, Dr. Hawks joined the faculty of anthropology at the University of Wisconsin–Madison. He teaches courses across the whole range of students, from freshmen to graduate students. The subjects range from large undergraduate introductory courses in biological anthropology to more specialized topics in human evolution and anthropological genetics.

Dr. Hawks has been awarded several grants for innovation and use of technology in his teaching. His courses have included online collaborative writing projects and computer-based laboratory exercises in genetics. He has incorporated 3-dimensional imaging technology in his fossil bone labs, allowing introductory students to have access to the best-quality research data. Dr. Hawks has mentored independent research projects for dozens of undergraduates. His graduate students have had notable successes in presenting and publishing research and winning grants to support their work.

Early in his career, Dr. Hawks focused mainly on fossil and archaeological evidence for our evolution. But as the Human Genome Project was completed, he became one of the first paleoanthropologists to use genetic and fossil information together to test hypotheses about human prehistory. The genetic record has begun to yield new information about every period of human evolution, from our initial divergence from other lineages of apes up to the last 10,000 years. Dr. Hawks's research has examined this entire time span; he has published research papers on both the earliest possible human ancestors and very recent evolution in historic times. He is unique in the way he combines traditional study of fossil evidence with new approaches from genetics. His ability to draw on both kinds of analysis has led to new insights about our recent evolution.

Dr. Hawks's work on the last segment of our evolutionary history has achieved the most impact. He documented the accelerating pace of selection pressures on humans living after the advent of agriculture and connected the rate of change to the growth of human populations. Along with the modeling and analysis of genetic sequences, this study has included the study of Bronze Age and later skeletal samples from Europe, East Asia, and Africa. His work has taken him around the world to examine skeletal remains of both historic and prehistoric populations.

His work on Neandertals has also broken new ground in paleoanthropology. His work in theoretical genetics showed the substantial likelihood of interbreeding of humans and Neandertals, together with the conditions for recognizing Neandertal genes within contemporary populations. These predictions were later confirmed by the direct sequencing of DNA from ancient Neandertal bones. Together with his students, he is examining the function of Neandertal genes and the ways that human populations evolved across the last 50,000 years. His work in this area was featured in the National Geographic Channel documentary *Neanderthal Code*.

Dr. Hawks has become well known for writing one of the top blogs on science, where people can follow his descriptions of the latest science in paleoanthropology. His site is visited more than 7,000 times a day, and in any given month, his blog is read by people in more than 150 countries. He travels widely to lecture about human origins, has given hundreds of radio and press interviews on the topic, and is a *Science Saturday* regular for the online interview show Bloggingheads.tv. In 2010, The Great Courses released *Major Transitions in Evolution*, presented by Dr. Hawks and Dr. Anthony Martin of Emory University. ■

Table of Contents

INTRODUCTION

Professor Biography i
Course Scope 1

LECTURE GUIDES

LECTURE 1
Ramapithecus—Ape Man 3

LECTURE 2
Australopithecus afarensis—Ancestor or Not? 9

LECTURE 3
Ardipithecus—Hominin or Not? 14

LECTURE 4
Brain Structure versus Brain Size 19

LECTURE 5
The Dietary Hypothesis 25

LECTURE 6
Africa or Asia? 30

LECTURE 7
An Ape's View of the Oldowan 34

LECTURE 8
Who Was *Homo habilis*? 38

LECTURE 9
How Big Was *Homo erectus*? 42

LECTURE 10
The Movius Line 46

Table of Contents

LECTURE 11
The Hobbits of Flores 51

LECTURE 12
Archaeology and Cooperation 56

LECTURE 13
Presapiens or Preneandertal? 61

LECTURE 14
What Do Stone Tools Reveal about Early Man? 66

LECTURE 15
Did Neandertals Speak? 70

LECTURE 16
Neandertals—Extinct or Ancestors? 74

LECTURE 17
Is Our Neandertal Heritage Important? 79

LECTURE 18
Multiregional Evolution versus Out of Africa 83

LECTURE 19
Climate's Impact on Our Evolution 88

LECTURE 20
Language—Adaptation or Spandrel? 92

LECTURE 21
Why Did Humans Start Creating Art? 97

LECTURE 22
Clovis or Pre-Clovis? 101

LECTURE 23
Farming—Migration or Diffusion? 106

Table of Contents

LECTURE 24
Are Humans Still Evolving? 110

SUPPLEMENTAL MATERIAL

Timeline 115
Glossary 121
Bibliography 132

The Rise of Humans: Great Scientific Debates

Scope:

The study of human evolution is changing. Most paleoanthropologists were once drawn from the field of anatomy. They studied how the human skeleton compared to other primates and ancient fossil remains. Archaeologists studied how the stones and animal bones left by ancient people might relate to their behavioral patterns. Today, these traditional kinds of evidence are just the beginning of our examination of the past. Microscopic features of bone, teeth, and ancient soils preserve evidence of ancient foods, growth rates, and cultural practices. The chemical composition of fossils can tell us what ancient people ate and how that changed over time. Most strikingly, we now have genetic evidence from ancient skeletons themselves, giving us a window on biology and behavior far beyond the skeleton. It is an exciting time, and even specialists have trouble keeping up with these advances.

Still, despite this huge shift in the evidence for our evolution, many of the basic questions of human origins remain the same. How did one lineage of ancient apes come to walk upright, on 2 legs? What explains our unique brains, with cultural and technological prowess unparalleled in any other species? Did ancient people have social lives like ours, talking and cooperating, or were they somehow different? And has our evolution stopped, or is it still going strong?

This course examines those questions through the lens of great debates that have shaped the study of our origins. Many of these are the burning questions of today's scientists: Did Neandertals speak? What explains the unusual skeleton known as the "hobbit"?

The lectures present 24 debates in human evolution. Each lecture sets the sides of the debate in their historical context. The history of many of the debates revolves around some of the main players in the history of paleoanthropology, and the course explains how these characters shaped the growth of the science. As the history unfolds, each lecture brings traditional sources of evidence up to date, discussing the latest fossil discoveries, new findings from genetics, and the importance of new methodologies for progress on old problems. Genomics, anatomy, and archaeology all emerged from the same history, and scientists work to find the explanations that can fit all these kinds of data.

These debates were central to decades of scientific research. Can we reconstruct cultural systems from the stones and bones they leave behind? Did modern humans originate in Africa recently, or did our origins involve other continents as well? Why can't apes learn the structure of human language? In each case, researchers have dedicated entire careers to the answers—sometimes bringing us closer to the answer, but often finding new mysteries along the way. ■

Ramapithecus—Ape Man
Lecture 1

***Ramapithecus* was cast out of our ancestry by molecular comparisons that indicated that our origin from a chimpanzee-human common ancestor must've been more recent than *Ramapithecus* lived. But it was ultimately cast out by fossil comparisons showing that this exceptional fossil, which was believed to be part of the human family tree, actually was part of another family tree. The paleontological debate that had ensued over 70 years was ultimately resolved by drawing together these different pieces of evidence.**

The debate about whether *Ramapithecus* is our ancestor is a debate that involves many sources of evidence that come from very different areas. Anatomically, fossil remains from *Ramapithecus* are similar to humans in some respects and different in others. Genetically, we have been able to determine that *Ramapithecus* is not our ancestor by comparing different living primates to it.

Today, our understanding of evolution depends on fossil, skeletal, and genetic evidence—and in some cases, microscopic or chemical evidence—which are all difficult to keep up with. But when we look back through the history of the field, we find that the fundamental questions about how we're related to other kinds of fossil hominins and primates have been established from the very start.

> **Genetically, we have been able to determine that *Ramapithecus* is not our ancestor by comparing different living primates to it.**

Debates have always framed the study of our ancestry. **Paleoanthropology**, the study of human evolution, is an area of study that often takes decades to resolve questions. For this reason, paleoanthropologists are very clever in finding ways to connect their questions to other areas of science.

Ramapithecus was found first in 1932 by G. Edward Lewis, who was working in the Siwalik Hills of Pakistan. *Ramapithecus* is a South Asian form of fossil ape that comes from sediments from the late **Miocene** epoch, a time period that dates to between about 5 million years ago (the dawning of human evolution) up to as early as about 25 million years ago. However, when *Ramapithecus* was found, the dating was unknown.

Ramapithecus gives a very unique form of information—derived from the teeth and the jaw—that we see often in the fossil record. The jaw, the mandible, is the hardest bone in the body, and the teeth are even harder, so oftentimes jaws and teeth are preserved when nothing else is.

In 1961, Morris Goodman discovered that humans and chimpanzees are close relatives.

When examining the jaw of *Ramapithecus*, we discover that its canine, the fanglike tooth, is similar to a human canine in terms of its size. The jawbone that Lewis found lacked a canine, but it had a socket for the canine, so we could visualize the size of that tooth. In comparison to other kinds of primates, this distinct similarity is surprising.

Nobel Prize winner Linus Pauling and his student Mort Zuckerkandl first used molecular evidence to relate different species to each other in the early 1950s. They assumed that species become different from each other over time because their molecules are evolving. Today, we do similar kinds of molecular comparisons with gene sequences, where there's a dynamic that is not necessarily clear at the level of proteins or other molecular sequences.

The **neutral theory of molecular evolution** states that much of the human genome evolves in a way that is neutral—it can change one way or another without making much of a difference. When we do genetic comparisons today, we often do them in parts of the genome that we believe are neutral

Gorillas, while related to humans, are a more distant relative than chimpanzees.

because that allows us to get a more accurate point of view of gene mutation and how genes have changed over time.

In 1961, Morris Goodman began the first effort to resolve the trichotomous relationship between humans, chimpanzees, and gorillas by using molecular evidence. By analyzing the effect of an antihuman antibody on blood sera from these 3 mammals, he found that humans and chimpanzees are close relatives and that gorillas are more distant relatives.

At the time of Goodman's work, there was a revival in trying to work out the relationships to primates with more distant Miocene forms of primates. Elwyn Simons and David Pilbeam were inspired to reexamine the *Ramapithecus* sample and found that it was potentially similar to some African Miocene apes.

One African ape form, **Kenyapithecus**, was found by Louis Leakey and was estimated to be about 12 million years old. *Kenyapithecus*, like *Ramapithecus*, has a relatively small canine. A reconstructed version of *Kenyapithecus* shows jaws that are not that apelike; instead, it might be a relative of early humans.

By the late 1960s and early 1970s, radiometric dating, in which people determine the age of rock deposits that have layers of volcanic ash, showed that *Ramapithecus* was more than 10 million years old and that *Kenyapithecus* was 12 to 14 million years old. If those 2 forms were related to humans, then humans and African apes must have diverged earlier than 10 to 14 million years ago.

Primatologist Clifford Jolly created a model that attempted to explain the differences between humans and our ancestors, early **hominins**, and our differences from apes in terms of diet. His proposal was that smaller canines, larger molars, and shorter snouts were all products of needing to chew a lot. **Bipedality**, walking upright instead of walking on all fours like apes, came as a side effect based on using hands to manipulate seeds.

During the early 1970s, **molecular clock** comparisons became much more detailed. People began to determine not only which primate is our closest relative, but how long ago we diverged from chimpanzees compared to how long ago we diverged from gorillas, orangutans, and other earlier kinds of primates.

In 1974, Berkeley scientists Vince Sarich and Allan Wilson used this molecular clock dating technique to determine that no fossil earlier than 8 million years old could be a hominid no matter what it looked like—a direct challenge to the paleontologists, but they were right.

More excavations in the Siwalik Hills showed that there were abundant remains of another kind of fossil ape called ***Sivapithecus***, which was larger than, and turned out to be a male version of, *Ramapithecus*. In paleontology, when there are 2 kinds of primates living in the same time period in the same place and one of them is consistently smaller than the other, they are the male and female versions of the same species.

Sivapithecus is an Asian ape, and Asian apes diverged from the African apes early in the Miocene. Those Asian apes are the ones that gave rise to today's orangutans, but they have nothing to do with human ancestry—they are a side branch to our family tree. Therefore, *Ramapithecus* is not a human ancestor.

An exciting part of being a paleoanthropologist is knowing how the history and the debates have unfolded over time, drawn in new sources of evidence, and given us new perspectives on our relationships with other kinds of primates. ∎

Important Terms

bipedality: walking on 2 legs.

hominin (a.k.a. **hominid**): a member of the human lineage, more closely related to living people than to chimpanzees or other living primates. This group was formerly called the "hominids," but "hominid" now technically refers to humans, chimpanzees, gorillas, and their relatives. Living and fossil apes, including chimpanzees, gorillas, gibbons, orangutans, and humans are called hominoids.

Kenyapithecus: fossil ape that is 14 million years old and was discovered by Louis Leakey in 1961 at a site called Fort Ternan in Kenya.

Miocene: geological epoch that extends from about 23 to 5.3 million years ago. It was a time of warmer global climates, when as many as 100 species of apes roamed throughout the Old World.

molecular clock: technique in molecular evolution that infers the time that species diverged from each other based on the amount of genetic difference and the rate of molecular change over time.

neutral theory of molecular evolution: theory that the vast majority of evolutionary changes at the molecular level are caused by a random drift of mutations that are not under selection.

paleoanthropology: study of ancient humans.

Ramapithecus: fossil primate genus that lived around 10 to 8 million years ago and was once thought to be the first direct ancestor of modern humans but now recognized as a synonym of *Sivapithecus*.

Sivapithecus: fossil primate genus dating from the Miocene Epoch (23.7 to 5.3 million years ago) and thought to be the direct ancestor of the orangutan.

Suggested Reading

Wolpoff, "*Ramapithecus* and Hominid Origins."

Questions to Consider

1. Which kind of evidence is more useful in guiding us to form hypotheses about evolution—fossils or genetics?

2. The lecture discusses museum exhibits, where fossils are easy to illustrate, but genetics can be more challenging. How might a problem like *Ramapithecus* be presented in a museum setting?

Australopithecus afarensis—Ancestor or Not?
Lecture 2

Australopithecus afarensis **looks like a good ancestor for all later hominins. The reason to accept an earlier *Homo* ancestor has mostly disappeared with redating. But *Kenyanthropus* raises the possibility of diversity at the time of *Australopithecus afarensis*, and if there were multiple species, only one could be our ancestor. We still don't know whether *Australopithecus afarensis* is our ancestor or a side branch of our human family tree.**

One of the most classic cases in the study of evolution in which the personalities of the scientists have become really involved in the way that the debate progressed is a debate between 2 of the most famous paleoanthropologists, Don Johanson and Richard Leakey, about the status of one species, *Australopithecus afarensis*.

Australopithecus is a genus that represents an earlier, entirely extinct form of a humanlike creature. There are several different species of *Australopithecus*, and they were found first in South Africa in the 1920s. The earliest varieties lived around 4.2 million years ago, and the latest forms lived around a million and a half years ago.

Australopithecus is a genus that represents an earlier, entirely extinct form of a humanlike creature.

Compared to humans, *Australopithecus* was always smaller than the smallest humans in normal-size populations and didn't have a very humanlike brain or behavior. In many respects, it was much more apelike than any of the representatives of our own genus, ***Homo***.

Where does this early hominin fit into the human family tree? One hypothesis is that it may be an intermediate between us and apes; it may be our ancestor. But the alternative point of view is that it's not our ancestor; it's a side branch of our evolution.

Is *Australopithecus afarensis* our ancestor, or is it a side branch of our evolution? The 2 men most directly involved in this question, Richard Leakey and Don Johanson, had rival sets of fossils. In terms of anatomy and of dating, there existed a rivalry between Don Johanson and his team, who found *afarensis*, and Richard Leakey, who found a skull called ER 1470, which he found on the east side of what is now Lake Turkana in Kenya.

Australopithecus afarensis was thought to be about 3.2 to 3.4 million years old; ER 1470 was initially thought to be about 2.6 million years old. These 2 things could be an ancestor and a descendent—and all of them ancestors of humans—except for the disagreement of Richard Leakey, who thought that *afarensis* didn't make a good ancestor for his fossil ER 1470.

During the early 1970s, Laetoli in Tanzania was the earliest site at which any fossils that were plausibly related to us had been found. Laetoli represents a fossil landscape that existed about 3.6 to 3.5 million years ago, the very earliest stage known in our evolution. Today, we know that human evolution may have begun quite a bit earlier than this.

Laetoli is a site that contains the fossilized footprints of an ancient group of hominins. These footprints track along for many dozens of meters making very distinct trails. The anatomy of these footprints shows that these creatures were fully bipedal and their feet had the main features ours have.

The footprint site is not the only aspect of Laetoli that was of great interest to paleoanthropologists—maybe more important are the fossil remains themselves. The most famous of these is a fossil mandible, a jawbone, called LH 4, which stands for Laetoli hominin 4. LH 4 is an important specimen because it became the type specimen, which means it stands in as a representative of its species, of *Australopithecus afarensis*.

The jawbone of *Australopithecus afarensis* is not in between that of chimps and humans. It is humanlike in some respects, apelike in some other respects, and completely different from both in one respect: the size of their teeth resulting from the thickness of the enamel.

The debate that ensued over *Australopithecus afarensis* began with Mary Leakey, Richard's mother, who was excavating at Laetoli. Because she was not an anatomy specialist, she brought in a young anatomist from the United States, Tim White, who later became very famous for many fossil discoveries.

To understand the anatomy of the Laetoli fossils, White wanted to compare them to those found at other fossil sites around Africa. Hadar, in Ethiopia, was one of the most exciting sites that was producing new fossils of *Australopithecus* and was where, beginning in 1973, Don Johanson was finding fossil evidence of another kind of *Australopithecus*.

Johanson and White brought their fossils together, decided that the teeth and jaws represented a single kind of hominin, and named it *Australopithecus afarensis*. They felt strongly that their 2 samples should be in the same species, so they set up LH 4 as the type specimen of *Australopithecus afarensis*. Although Mary Leakey had found LH 4, these 2 published the name and informed her later.

Mary was furious about this naming because according to the rules of **taxonomy**, or the classification and naming of organisms, when you name a species, you assign the name to a type specimen, and that name has to stick to the type specimen. Somebody can't come along later and call that type specimen some other species unless they get rid of the first one entirely.

Therefore, *Australopithecus afarensis* is the assigned name, but is it our ancestor? This question was taken up by Mary's son Richard, who was excavating on the east side of Lake Turkana. In 1972, a member of his field crew, Bernard Ngeneo, found what has become one of the most important fossils in the entire fossil record, a skull called KNM-ER, which stands for Kenyan National Museum-East Rudolf 1470.

The 1470 skull is big brained, like *Homo*, and was found under a stone layer that was believed to have been laid down 2.6 million years ago. Richard proposed the possibility that there would be some earlier form of *Homo* that they might yet find that had been living at the same time as *Australopithecus afarensis*.

In recent years, Maeve Leakey, Richard's wife, has been running the Turkana field site, and in 2001, she found a fossil skull on the west side of Lake Turkana that was the same age as *Australopithecus afarensis* but that shared some facial details with the 1470 skull. She called this new skull **Kenyanthropus**, a possible ancestor of *Homo*.

Because this new skull looked like the 1470 skull, Tim White began a debate by claiming that the skull was too badly preserved and wasn't clearly different from *Australopithecus afarensis*. In other words, the same scientists who began this debate in the 1970s are still carrying it on today.

Whether *Australopithecus afarensis* is our ancestor is still a mystery, and we won't know until new fossil discoveries uncover another species that's closer to us. ■

Important Terms

Australopithecus: genus of ape on the ancestral line leading to humanity.

Australopithecus afarensis: hominin that existed 3.9 to 2.9 million years ago ("Lucy") and was discovered by Tim White and Don Johanson at Hadar, Ethiopia, in 1978. Originally thought to be ancestral to modern humans, this hominin is gracile, bipedal, and has a small brain.

Homo: genus that includes modern humans and extinct species such as *Homo habilis* and *Homo erectus*, which are closely related to humans. This genus is descended from *Australopithecus* and is estimated to be about 2.3 to 2.4 million years old.

Kenyanthropus: hominin fossil that existed 3.5 to 3.2 million years ago and was discovered in Lake Turkana, Kenya, in 1999 by Maeve Leakey's team.

taxonomy: science dealing with the identification, naming, and classification of organisms.

Suggested Reading

Johanson and Wong, *Lucy's Legacy*.

Questions to Consider

1. How important are complete skeletons to understanding the past? For what kinds of questions might sets of fragments actually be more useful?

2. Why do paleoanthropologists focus so closely on finding ancestors of humans, as opposed to understanding the diversity of ancient species?

Ardipithecus—Hominin or Not?
Lecture 3

Tim White and Owen Lovejoy claim that *Ardipithecus* is the earliest well-understood member of our lineage and that it redefines how we understand both early hominins and our common ancestors with chimpanzees. Critics believe that *Ardipithecus* is some other kind of ape, not a hominin, and that the common ancestors of humans and apes may have been similar to chimpanzees and other apes in their body plan.

In 1993, Tim White and his team found *Ardipithecus*—"pithecus" is Greek for "ape," and "ardi" means "ground" in the Afar dialect—at a site in Ethiopia known as Aramis. Although it didn't look like an impressive fossil because it was a piece of a jawbone that had in it one baby tooth, this tooth looked like the baby teeth of later hominins. At a million years older than Lucy, it could have been the oldest known hominin at that time.

When White's team returned to the site later, they made the most fabulous discovery: a nearly complete skeleton of the species *Ardipithecus*. That skeleton, along with other teeth and fragmentary remains of the species, was found across a long interval of space in the Ethiopian badlands, precisely where Lucy was found.

> **Up until the discovery of *Ardipithecus*, it was believed that when we talked about early hominins, we were talking about upright, walking apes.**

Ardipithecus has given rise to one of the biggest debates in today's paleoanthropology: Is this fossil skeleton a hominin, or is it some other kind of ape? For *Ardipithecus*, much more so than for most other potential early hominin species, it would seem we have the evidence to make that assessment, but there are aspects of the skeleton that make it really difficult to say for sure.

Up until the discovery of *Ardipithecus*, it was believed that when we talked about early hominins, we were talking about upright, walking apes. When we look at early fossils, the teeth are what give us clues as to whether they might be similar to us, but we really wait for signs of bipedality to say that they are hominins. At some point after we diverged from other living apes, our pattern of walking upright must've emerged, but until that time we could very well be looking at apes that are in fact closely related to us but haven't yet evolved that pattern.

With *Ardipithecus*, the evidence about locomotion is fairly clear. Its foot had a big toe that was opposable, that stuck out away from the other toes and could grip onto branches, which is a pattern that we don't find in any other kind of hominin. There are some aspects of the bones in the ankles that show that *Ardipithecus* was potentially supporting weight through those hind limbs to a greater extent maybe than living chimpanzees and gorillas do. Although

Ardipithecus **had a chimpanzee-like hand, but it did not have the adaptations chimpanzees have that enable them to support the weight of their body on their knuckles.**

it had a chimpanzee-like hand, its hands don't bear the special adaptations for weight support on the knuckles that chimpanzees and gorillas have. *Ardipithecus* had small canines, and this one aspect of its dental anatomy is most similar to hominins.

Ardipithecus is a skeleton that came from very loose sedimentary deposits; it was crushed extremely. It took White's team 17 years to assemble this skeleton, much like a jigsaw puzzle. Using a CT scanner, which uses X-rays to reconstruct a 3-dimensional shape, they were able to rebuild the base of the skull to determine that it very clearly does not have a kind of vertical posture in its hind limb.

Because *Ardipithecus's* pelvis was preserved, White's team was able to determine that although it could seemingly move around better than a chimpanzee, it doesn't have the bowl-shaped pelvis that later hominins do. Its pelvis does not curve around to the front to provide the attachment points for the muscles that enable humans to move in an upright posture. In this sense, it's not like chimps and not really like humans; it is like the pelvis of another ape that lived around 5 million years earlier called ***Oreopithecus***.

More than 50 years ago, *Oreopithecus*, a nearly complete skeleton, was found in Tuscany, which was part of an island that extended into the Mediterranean 8 to 10 million years ago. The island habitat, lacking in the kinds of terrestrial predators that existed on the mainland, gave *Oreopithecus* a unique opportunity to become more focused on getting around on the ground. For this reason, *Oreopithecus* had adaptations in its pelvis that looked like adaptations to upright posture. Potentially like *Ardipithecus*, *Oreopithecus* also had feet that were able to support more of its weight. However, because it existed over 8 million years ago, *Oreopithecus* is not our ancestor.

Genetics showed us that *Ramapithecus*, a much more ancient ape, was far too old to be one of our ancestors; however, *Ardipithecus* is much younger and is in a timeframe when molecular evidence seems like it's consistent with humans and chimpanzees diverging. This is probably the most active part of this debate because as we develop more and more information about the human genome and the genomes of chimpanzees, gorillas, orangutans, and other apes, we're not only finding out when those populations had genes that were diverging, but we're able to use more sophisticated models to try to figure out when their populations were diverging.

When we consider 2 species that diverged from each other, we have to consider that not only do they have genes that diverged yesterday at the time that the species started to separate, but also they have genes that already had diverged millions of years before. And when we look at today's genetic differences between 2 species, we have to try to work out what the variation was like in that ancestor.

The variation gives us a clue about the time, and the more variation there was, the more recently it looks like the 2 species would've diverged. When we do this exercise for a chimpanzee and human beings today, it looks like their populations may have diverged as recently as 4 million years ago, even though their genes have variations from much earlier in time. This is troubling in terms of *Ardipithecus* because at 4-1/2 million years old, it's too old now to be part of the human ancestor population and not the chimp's ancestor. It's just in that time frame when the molecular evidence and the fossil evidence seem to be giving us a mixed message. It looks like the molecular clock is still playing the same kind of role as it did with *Ramapithecus*. Genetic comparisons are providing hints that maybe *Ardipithecus* isn't our ancestor—maybe it's too old to be in the hominin lineage.

Certainly the anatomy tells us that if it's a hominin it must be an extremely early form of hominin, something that doesn't have the unique form of locomotion that we do today. But of course, the answer to this question is going to have to depend on getting more fossil evidence, understanding the patterns of anatomical **parallelism** that might've emerged in other kinds of apes, and whether *Ardipithecus* reflects the kind of evolution that is similar to those apes or to humans. ■

Important Terms

Ardipithecus: hominin that is 4.4 to 5.5 million years old. Arguably the oldest known hominin yet to be discovered, it is bipedal, has a small brain, and has a grasping big toe for climbing.

Oreopithecus: an ancient genus of extinct apes that lived around 10 to 8 million years ago on an ancient island that included parts of present-day Tuscany and Sardinia.

parallelism: the evolution of geographically separated groups in such a way that they show morphological resemblances.

Suggested Reading

Gibbons, *The First Human*.

Questions to Consider

1. Is there any limit to how long hominins might have existed without evolving to walk upright in a humanlike manner? How would we recognize them?

2. Many hominins are found in eastern Africa because of the geological preservation, but it also was a unique environment. How likely is it that other parts of Africa were equally important to the emergence of hominins?

Brain Structure versus Brain Size
Lecture 4

Humans have brains that are 3 times larger than those of chimpanzees and that differ in proportion in several ways. Differences in both size and structure probably contribute to human cognition. But *Australopithecus* had basically apelike brains that may have some structural features of human brains. Did these structural features allow some humanlike behaviors in these ancient hominins? Were increases in brain size necessary to cause the behavioral shifts?

The human brain is what separates us from other apes more behaviorally than anything else about our anatomy. However, there is very little evidence available for paleoanthropologists about the way the structure of the human brain has evolved. The topic of how much of our brain evolution is just an increase in size versus how much is a change in the structure of the inside of our brain in terms of affecting behavior goes back to the very beginnings of the field and has given rise to some of the most intense debates.

In 1923, Raymond Dart found 3 fossils from a site called Taung that are the first fossil evidence of humans or human ancestors from Africa: the jaw of a fossil ape, the face of a fossil ape, and the fossil of what we call an **endocast**, a natural cast that forms inside of the skull of a fossil organism.

The issue was whether this fossil, named *Australopithecus africanus*, was a human relative or a kind of fossil ape. Dart, after examining its anatomy, came to the conclusion that this is related to us; that it's a fossil hominin. His logic was partly based on the teeth, but rested his interpretation that Taung is a hominin largely on the brain—its size and structure.

The size of the endocast in the brain of *Australopithecus* was a little bigger than expected for that of a chimpanzee or a gorilla of the same age. But there was a more significant aspect of this specimen: a small moon-shaped groove in the back of the endocast called the **lunate sulcus**, which is found in human brains and separates the visual processing centers from the rest of the brain. The position of that groove in humans is quite low, which means that the rest of the brain has expanded. In chimpanzees, this groove is higher, more forward.

Dart's observations became a focus for debate in the 1980s, and 2 specialists, Ralph Holloway and Dean Falk, were on opposite sides. Holloway thought essentially as Dart did, that the lunate sulcus was in a lower position, which meant that the structure of the brain in this species was more humanlike. Falk thought that you couldn't really tell where the lunate sulcus was, that this groove was not it, and that it might have been in the chimpanzee-like position.

Chimpanzees have brains that are approximately a third of the size of human brains.

The division between humanlike and apelike structure has been tremendously important to the way that we understand the evolution of the brain. We know that the brain has rapidly increased in size later in human evolution within the past 2 million years, and we know that *Australopithecus* had brains that were relatively much smaller than human brains. But what we don't know is whether there were key changes to the behavioral or social structure of *Australopithecus* that would have pushed them into evolving humanlike functions.

If the brains of *Australopithecus* had actually changed in structure, it would give us a hint that maybe they were adapting to do something that was a little bit different than other apes and that might lead toward changes that occurred later in human evolution. If, on the other hand, it's mostly size that makes the difference to our brains, then most of the events that were of importance must've happened later in evolution than *Australopithecus*.

A human brain today averages about 1300 cubic centimeters. A chimpanzee brain averages less than 400 cubic centimeters, which is about 350 cubic centimeters—a third the size of our brains. However, it is important to remember that size and cognitive function do not clearly correlate. Instead, we can talk about the factors that might've caused selection on the size of the brain and about the ways that the brain might respond to pressures in the environment.

The earliest endocast of ***Homo habilis***, KNM-ER 1470, was found by Richard Leakey and is around 1.9 million years old. When Ralph Holloway studied this endocast, he noticed that there was a prominent location on the surface, in the front part of it on the left side, in a particular area that's known in humans today as **Broca's area**. It looked like that area was developed more than it was in other earlier hominins or in apes.

This is very interesting because Broca's area is one of the essential areas for speech in humans today. In order to talk for any length of an utterance, you've got to figure out how your jaws, larynx, and breathing system will interact, and in what sequence, to produce those words. This discovery tells us that the kinds of communication skills that humans have today might've been emerging in the very earliest forms of *Homo* and is also something that appears to be quite different from *Australopithecus*.

The australopithecines have brains that are a little bit bigger than chimpanzees, even though the sizes of their bodies are about the same. If they were doing the same things, we would expect that their brains would be about the same size. The fact that their brains are a little larger may mean that *Australopithecus* had some sort of behavioral adaptations that other kinds of apes lack, although it is less clear what those adaptations might be.

The expensive tissue hypothesis states that because brains are energetically expensive, they must pay for themselves with greater energy acquisition. Some anthropologists propose that a change in body composition helps pay for larger brains—with a reduction in the gut that occurs in species that

Costs of a Larger Brain

In order to have a larger, more developed brain, organisms have to pay the costs of having a larger brain, and those costs are 3-fold in humans.

- Development time: It takes a long time to build the kind of brain humans have, making those neural connections and pruning away unnecessary elements.

- Construction: To grow and develop, brains need protein, which helps shape the ability of primates' brains to fit their environments.

- Energetic cost: The brain is energetically expensive; it consumes 20 percent of the human body's oxygen, which is a continuous cost to keep the brain running that demands calories.

have higher-quality diets, including *Homo*. This suggests that brain size may usually be limited, creating pressure on the structure of the brain.

Australopithecus had slightly larger brains than other apes, and early *Homo* had larger brains than *Australopithecus*. Those transitions of size might have been driven by the behavioral ability to get higher-quality foods and by the anatomical changes that ultimately pay the way for them.

We still don't know where the lunate sulcus is in *Australopithecus*. The anatomical debate between the 2 experts, Holloway and Falk, might only be settled if another endocast is found that has tremendous preservation. When it comes to whether there are changes

For the initial brains of early *Homo*, we can say that the change in size was coupled with a change in structure.

in brain structure in *Australopithecus*, this also is relatively unclear. It seems plausible that the larger brains of *Australopithecus* compared to apes implies something, but we can't target that in terms of what parts of the brain might've changed. For the initial brains of early *Homo*, we can say that the change in size was coupled with a change in structure. ■

Important Terms

Australopithecus africanus: early hominid discovered by Raymond Dart near Taung in South Africa in 1924. It lived 2 to 3 million years ago in the Pliocene. Like the older *Australopithecus afarensis*, *Australopithecus africanus* is often classed as a gracile australopithecine because it lacks the very large jaws and teeth of the robust australopithecines.

Broca's area: region of the hominid brain with functions linked to speech production.

endocast: internal mold of the cranial vault, used in paleoanthropology to study brain size and structure.

Homo habilis: hominin that existed 2.3 to 1.4 million years ago and was discovered by Mary and Louis Leakey in Tanzania that used primitive stone tools (thus "handy man").

lunate sulcus: a crescent-shaped groove on the occipital part of the brain. In fossil endocasts, when it can be determined, it may serve as a potential marker of cognitive evolution.

Suggested Reading

Falk, *Braindance*.

Schoenemann, "Evolution of the Size and Functional Areas of the Human Brain."

Questions to Consider

1. Are there other groups of animals for which brain size seems to be an important factor underlying behavioral differences?

2. Human brains are very flexible learning devices and have enabled rapid cultural change in human societies. What might the role of culture have been in earlier hominins?

The Dietary Hypothesis
Lecture 5

The South African australopithecines, *Australopithecus africanus* and *Australopithecus robustus*, were recognized as being different mostly because of the larger jaws and teeth of the robust australopithecine. John Robinson proposed that the robust australopithecines lived in forests and ate leaves while the gracile australopithecines lived on the savanna and ate fruits. Later studies showed that this interpretation was incorrect—robust and gracile australopithecines lived in a similar habitat and ate similar foods. Then why are they different?

Although humans do not descend from *Australopithecus robustus*, commonly referred to as the **robust** australopithecine, we do descend from some other kind of australopithecine. The things that set them apart from other kinds of hominids alert us to the ecological variability that hominids were beginning to exploit as they evolved ultimately into *Homo*. The debate about robust australopithecines has to do with the reasons they have larger chewing structures overall than any other kind of hominin.

John Robinson, who studied the robust australopithecines and other hominids, came up with the theory that the difference between robust and what he called **gracile** australopithecines is explained by a diet adaptation. Robinson theorized that robust australopithecines consumed low-quality food, similar to gorillas, while the gracile australopithecines consumed high-quality food, similar to chimpanzees. In what he called his **dietary hypothesis**, he determined that there was a clear difference between these hominins in habitat, in diet, and therefore in many other kinds of capabilities. The opposite side of this debate is that when we're looking at the differences between these hominins, we're actually looking at their interactions with an environment and with the way they might have evolved to adapt to an environment that was shifting over time. This is a debate that frames our consideration of diet in hominins.

At the time that Robinson was writing about the robust australopithecines, it was not clear how they related in time to the gracile australopithecines. It seemed like the gracile australopithecines existed a little earlier, but it wasn't obvious how much earlier. This is a key problem when we consider the South African fossil record, which is very different from eastern Africa or other parts of the world where volcanoes produced ash layers. In South Africa, fossils are found in ancient caves that over time collapsed, became filled, and maybe even refilled in a different way. The study of these caves initially was very difficult; it was hard to work out what an archaeologist would call the **stratigraphy**, which is where the fossils belong in a sequence.

Today, we have a pretty good idea of the way that these caves were formed because of C. K. Brain, who worked at a cave in South Africa called Swartkrans that is composed mostly of robust australopithecine fossils that are over 1.4 million years old. Brain specialized in looking at **taphonomy**, which is the study of everything that affects the surface and structure of a fossil after the organism died. In addition to finding fossils from robust australopithecines, Brain found bones of leopards and of their prey. The accumulation of these bones occurred in many distinct episodes due to the chamber opening and closing at various times, which created a tremendously complex stratigraphy.

> **Today, we have a tremendous source of evidence about the diets of these fossil animals by looking at the chemistry out of which their teeth are made.**

The skull of a robust australopithecine has a tall face that's relatively vertical, unlike other kinds of hominids that have a face that slopes forward to a much greater extent. When looking at the skull from the front, we see tremendously wide cheekbones that are the roots of chewing muscles called the masseter muscles, which are weak in humans. Although the front teeth, canine teeth, and incisor teeth are very small, the premolar teeth are very large and have a molar shape. The molars are sometimes truly massive, which causes a large surface area that is made for grinding. With these early hominins, we find fossil jaws that have these teeth worn down to nubs—they were using them to chew on things that took that degree of wear.

Gorillas today do not have giant molar teeth that are made to grind against each other; they have teeth like scissors that interlock, allowing them to cut apart leaves and other high-roughage foods. Robust australopithecine teeth would be miserable for eating this kind of food. From this standpoint, Robinson's analogy begins to fail. At the time of these hominins, the world's climate was drying, and Africa was becoming less forested. These roughage-eating hominins could not survive in such a climate.

Gorillas have the ability to eat high-roughage foods like leaves because their teeth interlock like scissors and easily cut the leaves apart.

Today, we have a tremendous source of evidence about the diets of these fossil animals by looking at the chemistry out of which their teeth are made. We can take samples of teeth and actually determine the ratios of different kinds of elements in them. Some of those elements are really informative about the types of food that were eaten, and some can be chemically substituted for each other. Carbon, for example, occurs naturally in different isotopes, which are forms of an element that have the same number of protons in the nucleus of each atom but a different number of neutrons.

When you look at the ratio of carbon 13 to carbon 12, you're really getting an assessment of how much of an animal's diet was rooted ultimately in grass. It turns out that robust and gracile australopithecines were very similar; they ate a lot of plants and some animals, but about 25% of their diet was grass. Therefore, these early hominins were potentially making use of very similar resources to early humans and also to chimpanzees, who are browsers that eat a lot of insects. In robust australopithecines, scratches found by archaeologists on their bones seem to be due to digging into termite mounds.

When examining robust australopithecines, we see a dietary adaptation which is interestingly flexible—but why the need for large teeth made for grinding? When we think about a diet, we have to consider not only the day-to-day diet, but also how that diet might evolve over long periods of time. Today, we can use a laser to take samples of isotopes from different parts of the same tooth to determine the ratios of carbon 13 to carbon 12 that might have changed with changes in the animal's diet over time.

One robust australopithecine tooth from Swartkrans shows that the diet did change in this animal over the course of about a 2-year span of its growth and development, which probably means that they were trying hard to survive in a changing climate and had the teeth and jaws that gave them that flexibility. The notion that they were able to fall back on lower-quality foods, which gave them a survival advantage that our ancestors may have lacked, is known as the **fallback food hypothesis**, which is widely accepted.

Overall, this is not a straightforward story in which the robust australopithecines were eating one thing and the gracile australopithecines were eating something else. Instead, they were eating the same range of foods, but as the climate shifted and as they were forced into more specialized roles by other kinds of creatures, they had to specialize in a way that would give them that fallback potential. ■

Important Terms

Australopithecus robustus: fossil hominin that is 2.3 to 1.3 million years old and was discovered by Robert Broom in South Africa in 1938. Its jaw musculature, mandible, and teeth are larger than *Australopithecus afarensis* or *Australopithecus africanus*.

dietary hypothesis: the hypothesis that gracile australopithecines had access to higher-quality food sources such as fruit and meat, while robust australopithecines were confined to lower-quality foods such as roots and grasses.

fallback food hypothesis: the hypothesis that in times of plenty, gracile and robust australopithecines both had access to high-quality food sources such as fruit and meat, but in scarcity, robust australopithecines used lower-quality foods such as roots and grasses as a "fallback" diet, while gracile types looked harder for fruit and meat.

gracile: hominins having a smaller skull, a slender bone structure, and teeth suited for tearing meat.

robust: hominins having a larger skull, a larger bone structure, and teeth suited for grinding seeds and nuts.

stratigraphy: study of the archaeological layers that make up an archaeological deposit to better understand the chronology and relationship of its artifacts.

taphonomy: study of decaying organisms over time and how they become fossilized (if they do).

Questions to Consider

1. If scientists studied a random sample of humans today using the methods of paleontology, what might they conclude about human diet?

2. Have new methods of analysis tended to reject earlier hypotheses about diet in early hominins, or have they merely added more detail?

Africa or Asia?
Lecture 6

Darwin hypothesized that humans are close relatives of the African apes, suggesting that Africa may have been the center of origin of ancient humans. But many of his contemporaries believed that Asia should be the center of human evolution. Fossil hunters used these theories to search for evidence of human origins—finding it first in Asia, and later in Africa.

The debate over whether Africa or Asia was the real heartland of human origins began with Charles Darwin, who believed that early man had originated in Africa and had spread from there to the rest of the world. He compared humans to African and Asian apes and concluded that we're closely related to chimpanzees and gorillas, the African apes, and we should come from the place where our relatives lived, Africa.

However, the earliest evidence of ancient humans was continually found in Asia or Europe—not in Africa. At around 1920 to 1930, elaborate theories arose to explain why Asia seemed to be the heartland of humanity. Today, new discoveries have put a new perspective on this debate; however, the most recent fossil discoveries still leave us wondering.

The Darwinian point of view about human origins was that the mode of our evolution involved changes first in the brain and consequent changes in the rest of the skeleton, including changes that occurred due to tool and weapon use, which then gave rise to bipedality. Therefore, when people were looking for fossil evidence of ancient humans, they were looking for something that had an apelike face and skeleton but a humanlike skull. Interestingly, the very first evidence of fossil humans, **Neandertals** from Europe, seemed to fit this pattern.

In Germany, the most popular evolutionary theorist was named Ernst Haeckel, who thought that humans might be more closely related to Asian apes, like the orangutan or gibbons. Haeckel and other evolutionary theorists at the time were faced with the problem of explaining why apes existed in

Southeast Asia, on islands like Sumatra and Borneo, and in Africa, but not elsewhere. Before we had a theory of continental drift, the only way people theorized that organisms traveled from one place to another was by sunken land bridges. So the theory of Lemuria, which is where Haeckel thought ancient humans should be found, was that there was a land bridge that was originally in the Indian Ocean that had sunk. These ideas persisted long into the 20th century, even though it turned out that Lemuria never existed.

In 1891, a young Dutch physician named Eugene Dubois found a skullcap (top part of a skull) and a femur (thigh bone) in Java, later called the **Java Man**, that he believed were part of the same human from a site called Trinil. Although Dubois was looking for something that had a humanlike brain and an apelike body, he interpreted these fossils as the evidence of something in between humans and apes—something that was upright in its stance but that had a more apelike skull. This missing link between humans and apes, what he named *Pithecanthropus erectus*, is now known as *Homo erectus*. The importance of Asia seemed to be established.

The American paleontologist Henry Fairfield Osborn believed that Central Asia would be the homeland of humanity. In his view, migrations from this area had spread across Asia and Europe repeatedly throughout history. His theory was the most widespread idea of **geographic determinism**, the idea that our population has features that reflect migrations from a single source.

Louis Leakey set out to show that Africa was the center of human evolution.

By the mid 1920s, Raymond Dart had found *Australopithecus*. Although features of his Taung specimen were more humanlike, its ape-sized brain seemed to counter Darwin's theory that large brains led the rest of our evolution. During the 1940s, more fossil evidence of *Australopithecus* was unearthed in South Africa. Before that time, Asia had looked like the real center point of our evolution, but very substantial finds began to make it clear that Africa was also important. Dart made further discoveries at a cave called Makapansgat that preserved evidence of *Australopithecus*.

Meanwhile, another paleontologist named Broom was finding evidence of *Australopithecus africanus* at the Sterkfontein cave and of the robust australopithecines from the Swartkrans cave. These fossil sites were tremendously important in reevaluating the pattern of our evolution because these sites were preserving much more primitive forms of ancient hominins.

Louis Leakey set out to show that Africa was the center of human evolution. His early discoveries were questioned because of doubts about Africa and about Leakey's ability to demonstrate that the sites were truly ancient. But slowly, his discoveries gained credibility. Ultimately, the discoveries at Olduvai Gorge, along with the South African fossils discovered by Broom and Dart, showed the ancient importance of Africa as the seat of human origins.

Presently, we have come to the conclusion that the earliest-known hominins are all African and that we are closely related to chimpanzees and gorillas, as Darwin had believed. The origin of the hominins is, therefore, probably African. Still, some scientists suggest that important events early in human evolution did happen in Asia. Most notably, some suggest that *Homo* may have come from Asia—as represented at Dmanisi, a place in the Republic of Georgia, where fossils were found of the oldest form known of *Homo erectus*. At 1.8 million years old, they are older than any clear evidence of *Homo erectus* inside of Africa.

Charles Darwin (1809–1882) hypothesized that all species have evolved from a common ancestor as a result of a process called natural selection.

The question remains: Did *Homo erectus* originate in Africa and spread very rapidly to Asia, or did it originate in Asia because some earlier form of hominin and australopithecine had left Africa and then evolved into something else? How these species spread from Africa to Asia—ultimately to Europe and other parts of the world—also still remains a mystery. ■

Important Terms

geographic determinism: theory that the human habits and characteristics of a particular culture are shaped by geographic conditions.

Homo erectus: species of hominin that originated in Africa—and spread as far as China and Java—from the end of the Pliocene Epoch to the later Pleistocene, about 1.8 to 1.3 million years ago.

Java Man: *Homo erectus* hominin that is 1 million years old and was discovered at Trinil, east Java, Indonesia, by Eugène Dubois.

Neandertal: fossil hominin that existed 150,000 to 30,000 years ago and were our closest extinct relatives. These hominins had large brains, used tools, and hunted and probably coexisted with *Homo sapiens*.

Pithecanthropus erectus: original name for Java Man, who is now considered to be *Homo erectus*.

Suggested Reading

Leakey, *Adam's Ancestors*.

Shipman, *The Man Who Found the Missing Link*.

Questions to Consider

1. What are the chances that we will find earlier evidence of *Homo* in Asia, even earlier than the Dmanisi fossil discoveries?

2. Are there other parts of the human past in which our interpretation of the past is really shaped by the places we happen to find evidence first?

An Ape's View of the Oldowan
Lecture 7

The first stone tools, approximately 2.6 million years old, are thought to represent a revolution in cognition and behavior. They were used for cutting and processing meat and animal carcasses, giving ancestral hominins access to this food with higher energy and protein. But chimpanzees make tools and hunt meat. Comparing early archaeological traces with the pattern of chimpanzee behavior leads some to conclude that early *Homo* may not have had any cognitive advances over those found in chimpanzees.

Toolmaking seems to be a fundamental aspect of what it means to be human. It is also a tremendously important aspect of the way that we study the fossil and archaeological past. Before the advent of durable stone tools that we find in the archaeological record, there is no archaeology. Those durable traces of ancient human behaviors give us a way to study how people interacted in the past with each other and with their environments.

Toolmaking seems to be a fundamental aspect of what it means to be human.

Today, we know that other kinds of primates also make and use tools. However, there's a clear distinction between them and us in terms of the materials used. Humans make tools out of stone, metal, wood, and other kinds of durable substances. Apes make tools out of wood, leaves, and other organic materials that don't persist in any kind of long-term archaeological record. The use of these different materials results in differences in the product, but is there a difference in the cognitive abilities that are necessary to be toolmakers?

Basic stone tools, which characterize **Oldowan technology**, so named because they were first identified and characterized at Olduvai Gorge, were often rocks found on the floors of river basins. They were heterogeneous because of the way they were smoothed or sharpened by the water. The earliest stone tools were manufactured by hitting one stone with a harder stone, a process that was later named hard-hammer percussion by archaeologists. Unmodified stones, or stones that have deliberate evidence of being used to hit other things but that are not shaped in any deliberate way, are an important aspect of the Oldowan archaeological record.

There is a basic division between different types of Oldowan tools: flakes, which are useful for cutting, **hammer stones**, which are useful for hitting with, and **choppers**, which are modified cores that can concentrate force. How do we know these were made by humans? Archaeologists look through the trash of ancient human behavior to determine the answer: They go to a place where ancient humans were making tools and excavate those tools to find small pieces of rock, most of which were not used by the hominins. They can then reconstruct what the form of the rock was that these things had been removed from, a process called refitting. Most importantly from this process, archaeologists can get a real picture of these hominins' cognitive features.

Hominins didn't just use the kinds of rock that they found at a particular archaeological site. By comparing modified stones, those that were actually made into tools, with unmodified stones, archaeologists found that hominins were selecting stones outside of the site and carrying them back to the site.

What kind of cognitive capabilities did these ancient hominins have? To answer that question we're going to have to turn to other kinds of primates. In 1960, Jane Goodall, who today is famous for her work with chimpanzees in Tanzania, discovered that chimpanzees in their natural environment were making and using tools.

The most famous chimpanzee tool that Goodall discovered is called the termite fishing, which is a stick that the chimpanzee has altered in some way. The chimpanzee takes that stick and inserts it into a hole in a termite mound or anthill, and after the insects have had a chance to attack it, the chimp pulls it out and licks them off. This is what a behavioral ecologist would call **extractive foraging**, or the process of taking a tool and modifying it to get food out of a context where they wouldn't have been able to get the food otherwise.

Probably the most complicated means of chimpanzee toolmaking, however, involves cracking nuts. Many chimps live where nuts are available, and nuts are a very rich energy resource. Some groups of chimps have developed means of getting into those nuts. They take either a log or a stone and put the nut on it, and then they use a hammer stone to beat the nut and get the nut meat out of it—a simple, logical process to a human. But for a chimpanzee, this is a highly technical process.

Suitable places to crack nuts are rare in the forest where chimpanzees live, so they have to find places that they can return to time and again to crack nuts. They also have to learn the hand-eye coordination to do this, which is a similar kind of process used to manufacture a stone tool. There's also deliberate teaching going on. That kind of cultural process is something that's very unique in chimpanzees, and that humans often take for granted, but it shows that the cognitive potential to develop this kind of technology exists in chimps.

The bonobos are close relatives of chimpanzees and live south of the Congo River. A bonobo named Kanzi was part of an experiment that was trying to teach bonobos how to use logograms, picture symbols, to communicate. As a juvenile, he was surprisingly good at identifying signs and making the connection between signs and objects. A group of archaeologists decided to see how much he could learn in terms of how to make and use a stone tool. He could hit rocks together and remove flakes (chipped off pieces) from them—and some of Kanzi's tools were very impressively similar to Oldowan-type technology—but what Kanzi discovered was that it's actually much easier for his anatomy to take a rock and throw it at the other rock, a skill he practiced and honed instead.

Early Oldowan technology was only out of reach of chimpanzees and bonobos for anatomical reasons—they don't have the hands for it. The earliest stone tools might not have taken advanced cognition as opposed to the kinds of technology that chimpanzees and bonobos are capable of. But *Australopithecus* did have hand anatomy capable of, if not well adapted for, working with stone. At least one site, Dikika in Ethiopia, housed bones that had distinct marks suggesting cutting and that date back as early as *Australopithecus afarensis*. ■

Important Terms

chopper: a rock from which several large flakes have been broken in order to produce a sharp edge or point. It is a characteristic tool of Oldowan technology.

extractive foraging: locating and/or processing embedded foods, such as underground roots and insects or hard-shelled nuts and fruits, with probes or other tools.

hammer stone: hand-held stone tool used as a prehistoric hammer to strike or fracture another object.

Oldowan technology: earliest stone tool industry in prehistory, being used from 2.6 million years ago up until 1.7 million years ago. Stones were shaped to be choppers, scrapers, and pounders and were used by *Homo habilis* and *Homo ergaster*.

Suggested Reading

Schick and Toth, *Making Silent Stones Speak*.

Wynn and McGrew, "An Ape's View of the Oldowan."

Questions to Consider

1. Why don't chimpanzees make and use flaked stone tools in their natural habitat?

2. Why is the transport of materials and resources so important to archaeologists as evidence about early hominin technology?

Who Was *Homo habilis*?
Lecture 8

> ***Homo habilis*** **was presumed to be the intermediate between *Australopithecus* and *Homo erectus*. Louis and Mary Leakey were its discoverers, and later their son Richard found more evidence of the species, which they claimed to be the first toolmaking species. But later discoveries challenged this hypothesis along 2 lines. First, even earlier stone tools and skeletons that don't have the large brains of *Homo habilis* have questioned the importance of the later sample. Second, *Homo habilis* might have persisted alongside *Homo erectus* for most of its existence, meaning that it probably is not the ancestor of this species.**

Homo habilis is one of the most famous of the fossil species of ancient hominins, and it has actually given rise to a surprising debate. *Homo habilis* seems to be the perfect transitional species between *Australopithecus* and the rest of our genus, *Homo*, but it doesn't clearly exist at the right time to have been our ancestor. Is *Homo habilis* genuinely part of the evolution of our genus, or is it possibly a side branch, a separate kind of species that originated from some earlier point in our evolution?

Homo habilis existed between about 2 million years ago and about 1-1/2 million years ago, long after *Australopithecus afarensis*. It's a time period during which early humans, *Homo erectus*, were emerging within Africa and Asia. Up to this point, we've been considering the anatomy of *Australopithecus*, which is shorter than us in stature but more or less comparable to us in width, had relatively big molar and premolar teeth, and relatively small brains. Otherwise, the anatomy is humanlike in its adaptation to upright walking.

When we compare this anatomical pattern to the pattern that occurs in later humans, we discover that humans have a more vertical face, a larger brain, smaller teeth, and a larger overall body size. These are the changes we expect to find at some point in human evolution if *Australopithecus* is to evolve into a humanlike form.

In 1960, Louis and Mary Leakey were searching for a potential common ancestor at Olduvai Gorge and found a fossil that today is numbered Olduvai hominid 7, or OH 7, which consists of parts of a skull, a jawbone, and a hand. These 3 parts of the skeleton are essential to being able to make the comparison between this fossil, later human fossils, and the earlier australopithecine fossils. This fossil represented something that was potentially in between the anatomy of *Australopithecus* and *Homo*.

Using the parts of the skull that were available, the Leakeys estimated that its size was in between the size of *Australopithecus* and *Homo erectus*. The jaw was also in between where you'd expect *Australopithecus* and later *Homo* to be. The post-canine teeth are where the real contrast was. *Australopithecus* has larger premolar teeth and larger molar teeth than we do. Olduvai hominid 7 had premolar teeth that were a little bit larger than ours, but not as large as *Australopithecus*.

Anatomist Philip Tobias and Louis Leakey discovered that the larger brain that these fossils represented was potentially very informative about the role of this species relative to the tools they found at Olduvai Gorge. They argued that this species was the toolmaker, that it was linked to us because of its large brain, and that the change in the brain and the consequent use of tools was necessary to reduce the size of the teeth. This hypothesis really laid the groundwork for their identification of a new species, which they called *Homo* "*habilis*," which means "able."

Is *habilis* a potential ancestor of *erectus* if it existed at around the same time as *erectus*?

The most famous specimen of *Homo habilis* today, however, is not any of the ones from Olduvai Gorge. It is a specimen called KNM-ER 1470, which we previously learned was from the east side of Lake Turkana. It has a very large brain compared to any of the other specimens of *Homo habilis* and a larger, flatter face that lacks a nose. Again, it's a skull that anatomically fits in between *Australopithecus* and *Homo*. KNM-ER 1470, when it was found, was excavated from a layer that was believed to be about 2.6 million years old, but later geological work revised the dating to be closer to 2 million years old. *Homo habilis* seems to be fitting into an early increment of the evolution of our genus but not much earlier than the known early specimens of *Homo erectus*, which creates the current issue: Is *habilis* a potential ancestor of *erectus* if it existed at around the same time as *erectus*?

What's clear among the *Homo habilis* discoveries of Lake Turkana is that there's a real difference between some of the specimens in terms of size to the point that many paleoanthropologists would call *habilis* a different species, **Homo rudolfensis**. Potentially, then, there are multiple species of *Homo habilis* that existed at the same time in eastern Africa, along with *Homo erectus* and *Australopithecus boisei*. Africa is beginning to look like a part of the world that has an incredible density of hominin diversity.

There's one major issue with early *Homo* that has created more of a puzzle than any other. *Homo habilis*—or *Homo rudolfensis*, if they're 2 species—have relatively larger brains than *Australopithecus* and an anatomy that's consistent with toolmaking. However, their body size is nothing like *Homo erectus* or later humans; it is essentially *Australopithecus*-like. Anatomists who have concentrated on this difference also concentrate on the notion that *Homo habilis* seems to have teeth and proportions that are unlike those of humans. They think that maybe this should be called *Australopithecus* instead because it is a better fit in an adaptive sense and that maybe we should look elsewhere for our ancestor.

One of the most important fossil discoveries to this *Homo habilis* debate was made very recently in South Africa at a site called Malapa. In 2009, Lee Berger excavated at least 2 relatively complete partial skeletons of a kind of early hominin that date to just around 2 million years old. The brain size of these skeletons is around the same size as the brain size of *Australopithecus africanus*, but their teeth are so much like the teeth of later *Homo*. This creates a contrast with what we expected to find: a large brain that would be consistent with the early evidence of tool manufacture. This hominin may be the ancestor of *Homo habilis*. What remains a mystery is whether that ancestor is also the ancestor of other later humans. ■

Important Term

Homo rudolfensis: hominin that existed 1.9 million years ago and was discovered by Richard and Maeve Leakey at Lake Turkana, Kenya. Many paleoanthropologists would view this as a synonym for *Homo habilis*.

Questions to Consider

1. What would human society be like if we had even greater differences in size between males and females, as some scientists think was true of *Homo habilis*?

2. Why might it be that *Homo habilis* and the robust australopithecines all became extinct before 1 million years ago?

How Big Was *Homo erectus*?
Lecture 9

> Fossils of *Homo erectus* are all consistent with larger body size than *Homo habilis* or *Australopithecus*. One exceptional skeleton from Nariokotome, Kenya, for many years has been interpreted as representing a very tall, slender physique for *Homo erectus*. Recently, that interpretation has been questioned both by comparison with other specimens and by a reevaluation of the process of growth in this species. Newer fossils from Dmanisi, Georgia, preserve a somewhat shorter model of *Homo erectus*, suggesting that the widespread dispersal of this species might have relied on hunting and gathering behaviors in addition to sheer size.

One of the most acrimonious debates in paleoanthropology is over a basic point of anatomy: the size of the *Homo erectus* body. For the past 25 years, we have thought that *Homo erectus* was characteristically a really large species in terms of its body size—that it not only contrasted with *Australopithecus*, which was small in body size, but that it also contrasted with more recent people in many cases.

The biggest piece of evidence for that is a skeleton from the west side of Lake Turkana called the Nariokotome skeleton, which is named WT 15,000 and referred to as the 15K skeleton in the field. It is the skeleton of about a 9- or 10-year-old boy who stood about 5'7" or 5'8" tall but had several more inches to grow. If this were the average for its species, then we would expect that *Homo erectus* was quite a tall species. But, in the last few years, further discoveries have sparked a debate because the people who originally found *Homo erectus* did not think it was especially large in body size.

The period of time between about 1.8 or 1.9 million years ago and about 1 million years ago encompasses the first evidence of *Homo erectus* in Africa, Asia, and on an island in Southeast Asia. At this point, this species is spread across at least parts of 2 continents. Much of the fossil evidence that we can recognize and identify is fossil evidence from the skull. Before

2 million years ago, the only hominins that we know definitely existed were australopithecines that were relatively small in body size.

Is *Homo erectus* really contrasting with *Australopithecus* in having quite tall bodies, or are they basically humanlike in size, which would be a much smaller increment of size increase compared to those earlier hominins? The earliest forms of hominins that we often put into our genus were, in fact, australopithecine-like in size. Those hominins coexisted with early *Homo erectus*, in addition to other upright-walking, bipedal creatures that were all small in body size: *Homo habilis*, *Australopithecus boisei*, and the robust australopithecine. There is some variation among them, some bigger individuals, but the question is: How much bigger were they?

The earliest fossils that can be attributed to *Homo erectus* within Africa are fossils that aren't diagnosable in terms of what their teeth and skulls look like. We call them *Homo erectus* because they're big. One example of this is a hipbone from the east side of Lake Turkana that is substantially larger than the hipbones—and, therefore, thigh bones—of any of the other known australopithecines, which cause us to estimate that some of them must've been quite tall. However, other thigh bones from the same deposits are actually quite short. On average, this type of fossil evidence made it seem like it was not a very tall species.

The Nariokotome skeleton is a fossil that we have relatively complete evidence about.

In eastern Africa, archaeologists had a problem for a long time: If they found a fossil thigh bone that doesn't have a jawbone or skull attached to it, there was really no way of telling which species it belonged to because all of the aforementioned species coexisted at the same time, in the same place. As a result, archaeologists have had a tendency to look at the skulls and determine that *Homo erectus* has a much bigger brain size, a much thicker skull, and much bigger anatomy to its skull than *Homo habilis*.

The Nariokotome skeleton is a fossil that we have relatively complete evidence about. Archaeologists assess age by using the clues to development that exist in a particular skeleton's long bones: thigh bones, shinbones, and the bones of the arm. In a process called ossification, the cartilage between bones keeps growing and keeps getting replaced by new bone within a body. By examining the extent to which this process has been undergone by an individual, archaeologists can determine age.

In the case of a fossil skeleton that did not grow in the same way as a living person when it was a living organism, we can compare the amount of bone growth to the amount of dental development that has occurred in the skeleton because different teeth erupt at different times. When we examine the teeth of the Nariokotome skeleton, they are actually relatively mature for an individual that is supposed to be 9 or 10 years of age, which might indicate that this individual was actually older. This basic disagreement—how much this skeleton has grown versus how much it has left to grow—is at the heart of many debates about the size of *Homo erectus*.

If the Nariokotome skeleton really was bigger than *Australopithecus*, it would have longer legs, which makes a difference in how far it can walk with a given energy input. It also impacts how big a range that can be covered when looking for food. In making these comparisons, we discover that early *Homo* would've had many different aspects to its ecology than *Australopithecus* would have had, including an adaptation to a warmer African climate.

This was the prevailing picture of *Homo erectus* until very recently. At that time, we had a transition to discovering that there were actually some rather small skulls in eastern Africa and Europe that had *erectus*-like, not *habilis*-like characteristics. Unlike the Nariokotome skeleton, it's very clear that the Dmanisi skeletons, the earliest known fossils of *Homo erectus*, represent a much smaller stature, standing about 5 feet tall. Dmanisi skulls are strikingly like the eastern African and Javan evidence for *Homo erectus*, except that they have significantly smaller brains. There is no doubt that *Homo erectus* was a variable species; it appears that there were populations that might have varied in body size just as there are populations of humans today that vary in body size.

Homo erectus wasn't totally from the neck down, and there was still a lot of evolution that was going to happen in different aspects of its anatomy—in particular, to its pelvis. The contrast in size from *Australopithecus* and *Homo habilis*, which were smaller, to a humanlike body size, laid the groundwork for the adaptation of this species to a broader geography with what is probably a hunting-and-gathering type of adaptation. ■

Suggested Reading

Fischman, "Family Ties."

Walker and Shipman, *The Wisdom of the Bones*.

Questions to Consider

1. Think of the people you know. How many of them would you have to measure to arrive at a good idea of the body size of living humans?

2. Large size has many advantages, but the australopithecines and *Homo habilis* remained small. What are some disadvantages of large body size for a hominin?

The Movius Line
Lecture 10

> The Acheulean industry is based on large bifacial tools—chiefly, the hand ax. This industry was the height of stone technology from 1.5 million years ago up to 250,000 years ago across Africa, Europe, and West Asia. Bifaces are very rarely found east of India, though; some archaeologists believe the reason to be due to the notion that different species of humans were present there. Other archaeologists have sought ecological reasons for the difference—different tools applied to different problems.

On the east side of Eurasia, there are consistently different kinds of archaeological remains—and to some extent different kinds of fossil hominins—than occur in the western part of the human range in Europe, West Asia, and Africa. This division of east and west is one that is very difficult to explain and is one of the most mysterious aspects of our evolutionary history within the past million years. Why do we see consistent differences from place to place if the people were able to move so easily from one place to another?

That interesting aspect of the archaeological fossil record is most clear when we consider the time period between about a million and a half million years ago when most of the rest of the world in the west were using **Acheulean technology**. This type of technology is based essentially on large **bifacial tools**, which are large rocks that have been flaked on both sides. When a rock has been flaked on both sides, it makes a sharp edge all the way around to produce a teardrop-shaped object called a hand ax.

We know that differences in the east and west must've existed, but we are still trying to determine the cause for the differences we see. Maybe there were fundamentally different kinds of hominins that existed in the eastern and western parts; maybe they are 2 different species. Another scenario is that there's something different about the east and west that made these bifacial tools work better in different parts of this continent.

The split between east and west, later known as the **Movius line**, was first noticed by an archaeologist named Hallam Movius, who was working at European sites in the 1940s. When he traveled to western parts of Asia, he found these Acheulean hand axes; however, in the east, the hand axes were rare. Instead in the east, he found a different kind of technology known as **chopping tool technology**, which was based on simple flaking tools and making cores with sharp edges that become choppers.

In principle, a hand ax is a simple kind of artifact. It might've been used to disarticulate the limbs of animals or to skin a large animal. It's potentially useful for all kinds of things—including plants and wood—and is limited only by the fact that it's sort of a large object. There was a very intensive use of this technology at some places over a relatively short period of time, in an archaeological sense. Why is it that these tools are so common and important in one part of the world but not in the other part?

In principle, a hand ax is a simple kind of artifact.

People have speculated about whether hand axes might have had some other purpose that would've differed between these parts of the world. Some archaeologists argue that the main purpose of hand axes is to take down animals from a distance by throwing them. Perhaps the symmetrical shape was significant in some societies that they didn't have in others.

In China, fossils are collected from caves, ground up, and used as treatments for various kinds of disorders as sort of a homeopathic remedy. In the 1920s, a Canadian named Davidson Black began looking for fossils in drugstores in Beijing and discovered that many fossils were coming from a place called Zhoukoudian, or Dragon Bone Hill in Chinese. After Black died, a German scientist named Franz Weidenreich conducted the rest of the excavations, reconstructing and interpreting the fossils.

Weidenreich reassembled the fossils he found and made careful casts of them. Today, these casts (and the interpretations of them) are all that we have left of Weidenreich's discoveries, which became known as the **Peking Man** fossils. With the onset of World War II, and because of the fact that Weidenreich was Jewish, these fossils had to be packed and shipped to the

United States upon his evacuation from China. Unfortunately, the Peking Man fossils were lost either in the course of being taken to the port or were on board the ship, which was sunk by the Japanese. Alternative theories have been proposed, and this has become one of the great mysteries in science.

Weidenreich recognized that the features of these fossils were very similar to the features of *Homo erectus* fossils from Java. He erected a new species, *Sinanthropus pekinensis*, even though he saw these 2 samples as representing one species that had differences in different places. Weidenreich believed that those differences were consistent with the kind of differences we see between people now, racial differences. He also thought that a similar pattern of differences existed between eastern and western populations, but many have argued against this theory in recent years.

To conclude the issues surrounding the east-versus-west phenomenon, archaeologists believe that *Homo erectus* is what was found in the east, but that in the west is something that is potentially a closer relative to us, a species called **Homo ergaster**. For about 30 years, there has been a trend that interprets these species as truly distinct populations.

Regarding the reasons that bifacial tools are predominately found in the west and not the east, there seem to be many compelling explanations that involve ecology. The most direct of these explanations involves the natural distribution of bamboo across the Movius line, specifically in the differences between the Indian and Southeast Asian areas. Although bamboo tools are obviously not going to show up in the archaeological record, they have been found to be much more useful and easier to obtain than a tool made of stone. For this reason, bamboo tools replace stone tools as the main technology where available. In addition, the range of bamboo species roughly matches the Movius line.

Further evidence that reinforces the idea that distinct biological populations lived in eastern and western Eurasia was discovered in a specific genome sequence found in the Denisova Cave in Russia. The ecological explanation may be plausible, though: Hunter-gatherers in the east still use bamboo instead of stone for many cutting needs. But the very long persistence of Acheulean industries seems to demand a more persistent explanation. ■

Important Terms

Acheulean technology: archaeological industry of stone tool manufacture associated with *Homo habilis* from about 1.8 million years ago that is characterized by oval- and pear-shaped hand axes.

bifacial tool: stone tool sharpened on 2 sides and used as a multipurpose knife or hand ax.

chopping tool technology: stone tool-making industry producing sharp flakes and shaped core chopping tools that was prevalent in the Oldowan, but particularly in what are now China and Southeast Asia. This technology existed for about 1.5 million years without a significant change.

Homo ergaster: a name for African fossil humans that existed between around 1.8 to 1.5 million years ago and that may be an ancestral population for all later humans. Most paleoanthropologists would call these fossils African *Homo erectus*.

Movius line: theoretical boundary line across Eurasia separating Paleolithic hand ax industries in the west from those without hand axes in the east that was proposed in 1948 by Hallam Movius.

Peking Man: hominin that existed 770,000 to 230,000 years ago (*Homo erectus*) that was found at Zhoukoudian, near Beijing, by Davidson Black.

Suggested Reading

Boaz and Ciochon, *Dragon Bone Hill*.

Questions to Consider

1. In recent times, technology and trade have flowed rapidly east and west across Eurasia by the Silk Road and other routes. Why might this have been different in the Pleistocene?

2. One explanation for the Movius line is ecological—for example, the idea that hominins in eastern Asia used bamboo tools. Are there other examples of ecological barriers that made an important difference to human history?

The Hobbits of Flores
Lecture 11

The most burning debate in paleoanthropology during the last 10 to 15 years has been the identity of *Homo floresiensis*. The entire series of fossils represents an extremely small-bodied population with a small brain. Found together with indigenous animals such as pygmy mastodons, giant storks, and Komodo dragons, these "hobbits" seem to represent a unique population of humans isolated for a long time from the rest of humanity. Many scientists initially doubted this conclusion. Without further archaeological discoveries, it may not be possible to settle this debate.

One of the most exciting fossil discoveries of the past 20 years occurred at Liang Bua cave, which is on the island of Flores. At this site is the remains of a kind of hominin that is very different from what is expected to be found—a skeleton that is small in both body and brain. It is not an australopithecine because it is only about 18,000 years old. This skeleton and the other remains that are found on Flores have given rise to what is one of the most intense debates going on in paleoanthropology today: Does this skeleton represent an ancient population that was highly different from other populations of humans, or does it simply represent a developmental abnormality, a pathological variant of a modern human?

Flores is an island in the Indonesian island chain and is located in one of the parts of the world where, during the **Pleistocene** epoch when glaciers advanced over the northern continents, the exposure of the sea floor was most expansive because much of the water in the ocean was being bound up in glaciers that were covering Asia and North America. This island, along with its neighboring islands, has an animal population that's predominately Asian in character because they were able to move back and forth during the Pleistocene.

Flores is a large island. It has a lot of potential for animals to colonize it and establish large populations, but it was never connected to the Asian mainland or to the Australian continent. In between these 2 provinces are a number of islands that were never connected by land to either of them and that have a variable set of species that are determined by whether or not the species could swim there. It's an area of the world called Wallacia after Alfred Russel Wallace, who was a contemporary of Darwin and studied natural selection as related to the fauna found in this region. The Wallace line, as the boundary between differing fauna is now known, is influential in our understanding of where and why hominins might have gotten to Flores.

As early as a million years ago up to the past few thousand years, Flores was isolated, and it was never connected to any island other than Komodo, which today houses the Komodo dragon. On Flores, there were no large carnivores at all, but there were shrunken elephants and giant storks. These 2 islands have shared a very distinct fauna and that might help explain what these ancient humans might've been doing on this island.

A contemporary of Charles Darwin, Alfred Russel Wallace (1823–1913) observed that there were zoological differences in the archipelago that caused a boundary between species, which later became known as the Wallace line.

When examining this skeleton from Liang Bua cave—a skeleton called LB1—we find that it's *Australopithecus*-like in size, very short. The molars and the premolar teeth, however, are not the size and shape of australopithecine teeth; they're much more humanlike. Although the skeleton looks sort of humanlike, the hipbones are much smaller than those of most living people, but it also has a projection in the front of it that's very strong called the anterior-superior iliac spine. That projection is distinct in *Australopithecus* as well. It's not quite as distinct in living and recent people. Because of its overall pattern of **morphology**—its small size and, as it turns out, relatively big feet—people have nicknamed it "**hobbit**," but the scientific name for this skeleton is ***Homo floresiensis***.

Humans arrived on this island a million years ago, which is also when people were first reaching China and not long after people had reached Java for the first time. It was a time of intense dispersal, but what's different about the dispersal to Flores is that in order to get to Flores, the humans had to cross water. They had to get across the channels that separate Flores from Southeast Asia, even during low water times. It's not clear how they managed this dispersal.

On Flores, we find primitive tools that are sort of equivalent to the Oldowan-type flaking technology. It's the kind of technology that is very characteristic of the eastern part of the Asian mainland, and here it is on Flores. There are similar kinds of tools found in the archaeological deposits in the Liang Bua cave, so there's an argument of continuity. However, 18,000 years ago when the hobbit skeleton was living, modern humans were nearby, so this hobbit population probably encountered them.

On Flores, we find primitive tools that are sort of equivalent to the Oldowan-type flaking technology.

When examining this hobbit skeleton, there are certain developmental oddities that are not exactly what you'd expect, but the strangest part is its extremely small brain—it's more chimpanzee- and *Australopithecus*-sized. One possible explanation is rooted in pathology, that there's a developmental disorder that would make its brain small. This explanation is favored by many anthropologists.

This skeleton represents a population that has shrunken in size—that once had larger brains, but in the course of shrinking has gotten much smaller brains. Looking at the skeleton in that way, it becomes very difficult to say that there's any kind of developmental disorder that occurs in living people now that could explain all of the characteristics of this skeleton.

But at the same time, many of the features that this skeleton has actually do seem to match earlier kinds of hominins, namely *Homo erectus*, but not with living humans. Therefore, there is a possibility that this is *Homo erectus* that reached this island a million years ago and shrunk in size over the course of time.

The remaining problem is explaining the extent of this shrinking because, for the hobbit, what it looks like is that the size of the brain reduced more than the size of the body. We know that this was a small population because we've got multiple small individuals, but what we don't have is multiple small brains. What remains to be demonstrated is whether this particular island was the right context for humans to become something that's quite different.

Twelve thousand years ago, the archaeological record on Flores begins to change. After that point, we have no more evidence of the hobbits; we have a clear change in the archaeology. This seems to be around the time, maybe 12,000 to 10,000 years ago, that modern humans drove whatever was there to extinction—the legacy of these people is gone. We haven't yet recovered any DNA that would tell us clearly what their relationship to us might be, but this species does give us a hint about the kind of potential that humans might've had as they dispersed into new environments to adapt in really surprising ways. ■

Important Terms

hobbit: nickname for *Homo floresiensis*, a dwarf-like hominin living on the Island of Flores until about 13,000 years ago.

Homo floresiensis: dwarf-like hominins living on the Island of Flores until about 13,000 years ago.

morphology: study of the form and structure of organisms and their specific structural features.

Pleistocene: geological epoch that extends from about 2.6 million to about 12,000 years ago. At the height of the Pleistocene glacial ages, more than 30% of the land area of the Earth was covered by glacial ice; during the interglacial stages, probably only about 10% was covered. The animals of the Pleistocene began to resemble those of today, and new groups of land mammals, including humans, appeared. At the end of the epoch, mass extinctions occurred.

Suggested Reading

Morwood and Van Oosterzee, *A New Human*.

Questions to Consider

1. Why do you think the case of *Homo floresiensis* has generated so much controversy among paleoanthropologists?

2. If genetic evidence could be recovered from the Liang Bua skeleton, what would you expect it to look like?

Archaeology and Cooperation
Lecture 12

> One of the oldest debates in archaeology is whether ancient stone tools were used for hunting animals or scavenging remains killed by other predators. Human hunter-gatherers survive by sharing food, which requires cooperation and coordination of different strategies. Some Oldowan sites appear to represent places where many people gathered over time, but most occurrences of stone tools are very small scatters that represent only a moment in time. Some evidence suggests cooperation among ancient people—even fairly complicated social organization.

It's remarkable what we can tell from the archaeological or fossil record about the lives that individual people in the past lived. When we look into the past to interpret the events of human evolution, sometimes the little things can get lost, but there are many aspects of human behavior that are built out of the individual decisions that people make and how they interact with each other. Interestingly, we can interpret people's interactions with each other and show that the humanlike qualities of cooperation and compassion are present in the archaeological and fossil record.

It is in the skeletons of Neandertals that we find the richest evidence of what their lives were like. One very clear aspect of some individuals is the amount of wear they have on their teeth, and from this we find evidence of grinding. The way in which the teeth are worn down tells us many things, including that they used their teeth to strip and soften leather and to eat large chunks of meat. There is also evidence from the archaeological traces on the human skeleton that Neandertals were probably right-handed in a very much similar proportion to recent people being right-handed more so than left-handed.

We can also tell from the fossil record that some Neandertals lived catastrophic lives. The clearest example is a skeleton from a site called Shanidar, which is a cave in northern Iraq. The skeleton of Shanidar 1 tells us that one of its arm bones was amputated during the course of his relatively long life. From this fact, can we assume that other individuals in his group must've been giving him some compassion that allowed him to survive his injuries, and from that can we then assume that the Neandertals were a compassionate group?

When we think about human interaction, we need to consider the kinds of groups that are interacting. Groups of primates are varied in how many individuals live in a group and in what type of pattern they live in. Chimpanzees have a population structure that's called a fission-fusion society, which means that a group of 30 to 50 chimpanzees will occupy a home range area in which the group will divide into smaller task-oriented units. The entire community does fuse at certain points to do some kinds of social interactions.

Chimpanzees have a population structure in which a group of 30 to 50 will divide into smaller units assigned to specific tasks.

There is a pattern of cooperation among males in which multiple males live in the same area and defend their territory from incursions from other males and other groups. This pattern of group life is found in chimpanzees, bonobos, and other kinds of primates, and it's certainly within the capacities of any kind of hominin in terms of social interactions, but it hasn't been clear whether that kind of group living is actually present in the archaeological or fossil record.

The only clear case in *Australopithecus* where group living might have existed is a site called AL 333, which is in the Hadar area of Ethiopia. At this site, archaeologists found an interesting group of individuals all buried together—they found males and females of all ages. One of the key aspects of the AL 333 assemblage is that there are multiple adult males there. Although it's a unique instance, this is a case where it looks like hominins were living in groups the way that chimpanzees do.

Looking at the earliest stone tools at Olduvai Gorge, archaeologists tried to interpret what the scatter of stone tools meant in terms of how groups were using space. If we can show that there were those kinds of central places in the archaeological record, it would help to substantiate that these hominins were cooperating with each other in a humanlike way. The early excavations at Olduvai Gorge seemed to show that there were what is known as **living floors**, places where people gathered and shared resources, in which these hominins were making stone tools and bringing back animals to eat. However, though archaeologists found objects in a fairly restricted area, it is difficult to determine that the objects were all left by the same people because placement could vary over a long period of time.

But in at least one case, at the site called FLK Zinj, there was dense accumulation of artifacts that clearly had been carried to that site from different places and seemed to have accumulated at the same time. There were also animal bones that had clear evidence of cut marks on them, and those animal bones were transported some distance. We know this because when people kill an animal and carry the parts off somewhere to eat, they only carry the parts that are most efficient to transport—the parts that are the most meaty and have the least amount of waste.

Neandertal males were hunting very large mammals, and they had to cooperate in order to do this. Their technology was very rudimentary—they were using spears that they had to hold with their hands and thrust into an animal. Because of this, they either knew where the animal was going to go, or they had other members of their group working to drive the animal toward them for an ambush, which is a strategy that involved communication and cleverness to have different roles for people in the hunt.

Dmanisi is *Homo erectus*, so it was alive during an earlier timeframe than the Neandertals. The skull of a relatively old adult Dmanisi female (D 3444) was found that showed that, during the course of her life, she lost all of her teeth. Without artificial teeth, there was either access to food that could be consumed without a lot of chewing or somebody to process the food by cutting it into tiny pieces. From an archaeological perspective, it's difficult to determine whether this woman had help, but it's quite plausible that she did.

In Neandertal groups, we find clear archaeological evidence of cannibalism; there are sites where bones are broken apart and have cut marks on them, just as animal bones would've been cut apart and broken for the marrow. This type of evidence seems to be evidence against compassion and cooperation, but it can be interpreted instead as instances of desperation or ritual.

When it comes to interpreting compassion and cooperation in the archaeological record, archaeologists have come a long way toward demonstrating that humans in the past must've had elements of cooperation that supported their lifestyle and their ability to hunt and gather food. However, there are individual cases in human history where people interacted with each other in violent ways at some times and in compassionate ways at others. What remains to be shown is the extent to which that potential is translated into our behavior toward each other on average and how it might've affected our evolution. ■

Important Term

living floor: level of an archaeological site where humans lived, as indicated by a scatter of stone tools, animal bones, and other artifacts.

Suggested Reading

Arsuaga and Klatt, *The Neanderthal's Necklace.*

Leakey, *The Origin of Humankind.*

Questions to Consider

1. Why do archaeologists seem to be so cautious in attributing evidence to cooperation among ancient people?

2. What kind of physical evidence of cooperation exists within the material produced by living human societies?

Presapiens or Preneandertal?
Lecture 13

In the 19th century, many anthropologists doubted that Neandertals could really be human ancestors because they had specialized anatomical features that are not found in any living people—meaning that evolution from them to us would need to run backward. These anthropologists believed that a less specialized form of hominin must be our ancestor. A presapiens hypothesis suggested that a very ancient and modern form would be found. The preneandertal hypothesis held that the ancestor would be a less specialized form of Neandertal. The European fossil record was interpreted in light of these scenarios.

In northern Spain, there is a hill called Atapuerca near the city of Burgos that, in the 1800s, had a railway line that cut through it. Today, there's no rail that goes through, but there's still a big cut through the mountain that has produced a lot of evidence of ancient humans. In this hill are a number of caves, and one of these caves has yielded what has become the largest sample of fossil humans found anywhere in the world.

When paleontologists began exploring this cave, they found a pit and called it Sima de los Huesos, which means "Pit of the Bones." Underneath countless animal bones, paleontologists eventually found human bones, which we now know date to around 600,000 years ago, and they haven't yet reached the bottom of this pit. This site has become central to understanding the biology of early humans, especially those who reached Europe.

During the first half of the 20th century, most of the action in paleoanthropology was in Europe.

During the first half of the 20th century, most of the action in paleoanthropology was in Europe. During their explorations of this fossil record, amateur prehistorians began to try to systematize where different things came from and how old they were relative to each other, which was guided mostly by theories. In the **presapiens hypothesis**, many anthropologists believed that there was an ancient form of humans that was essentially like modern humans in many respects that had existed long ago in Europe.

The other theory, known as the **preneandertal hypothesis**, held that there were, instead, primitive humans that didn't have any of the specializations of today's humans but that also didn't have the specializations of the later fossil humans called Neandertals. These primitive forms of humans were our ancestors, but they were Neandertal ancestors, too.

The presapiens hypothesis was the brainchild of Sir Arthur Keith, who made a strong commitment to the reality of the **Piltdown Man** fossils, which we now recognize as a hoax. It was a human skull that had been taken from a medieval cemetery, so it looked old, but the hoaxer colored it with iron so that it looked even more ancient. In addition to this skull was a broken orangutan's mandible with chimpanzee teeth that were filed down to look like they were worn in a humanlike way.

The Piltdown Man fossils, which turned out to be a hoax, included the broken jaw of an orangutan and chimpanzee teeth.

Sir Arthur Keith, who reconstructed the fossil, showed that this fossil had a humanlike braincase and an apelike face, which fit Charles Darwin's theory of evolution and became a lens through which many paleontologists began to view the human fossil record—with an emphasis on the presapiens hypothesis. However, Franz Weidenreich, the discoverer of the Peking Man, and others were never convinced by the Piltdown fossil because it was clearly an ape jaw and a human skull.

Other kinds of fossils were found to support the presapiens hypothesis. At a site in France called Fontéchevade, a part of a skullcap was found that was interpreted as being quite modern and as dating to a time when it would've been a part of a potentially presapiens population. However, because it was broken, the anatomy was not clear. Also, we now know that it dates later than initially thought.

Another fossil that was interpreted as being presapiens-like was Swanscombe, an English fossil. The back of the skull of one individual was found, and it looked like a Neandertal's skull in many ways, but it didn't have the front of the skull, which would better confirm the similarities to a Neandertal. Even though it was missing a vital part of comparison, many people theorized that this was a modern skull, which reinforced people's viewpoints of a presapiens population.

When Louis Leakey went to Africa initially, he was looking for evidence of this presapiens population, but he wanted to tie it to Africa to show the importance of Africa in our early evolution. When he found the Kanam jaw, it was, in his view, a presapiens representative of a population that existed early in Africa that was of equal antiquity to the kinds of specimens that were being found in Europe. This extension of the presapiens idea was very influential on the way people set goals to look for new remains in Africa.

F. Clark Howell arrived at a different point of view about how Neandertals had originated and how they were related to us. To Howell, skulls like Ehringsdorf from Germany that are very Neandertal-like in many respects but not in all are preneandertal specimens. In his view, this particular skull hadn't yet gotten all of the specializations that later Neandertals would get.

Looking at this population, Howell thought that this might be a really good population to derive the anatomy of more recent humans from.

The most important site from around the 1950s was the series of caves that occur within Mount Carmel, Israel. These caves had been excavated during the 1930s by Dorothy Garrod, and the anatomy of the fossil specimens was later analyzed by Sir Arthur Keith and Theodore McCown. These 2 discovered that the fossils present evidence of one biological population that had a blend of traits from Neandertals and modern humans.

Keith and McCown compared these fossils and hypothesized that this is a population in the throes of evolution. Surprisingly, they believed that this population was evolving from a presapiens form into a Neandertal form.

Geneticist Theodosius Dobzhansky looked at these fossils and determined that this was a population of hybrids—these hominins were a mixture of Neandertals and modern humans. This perspective is similar to what modern theorists might say about these samples.

Atapuerca, a site of dominant importance today for many reasons, contains hominids that were evolving toward a Neandertal anatomy and are called *Homo heidelbergensis* because of the similarities in their skulls. This is a population that shows us what the first inhabitants of Europe were like.

Both the presapiens and preneandertal models were wrong. Every ancient skeletal individual claimed as evidence for a presapiens population has turned out either to be less modern than originally claimed or was misattributed to much more ancient dates than we now accept. Genetics now points to a common ancestry for humans and Neandertals between 250,000 and 400,000 years ago, which would imply that many of the preneandertal fossil specimens in Europe are too old to be Neandertal ancestors. ∎

Important Terms

Homo heidelbergensis: hominin that existed between 600,000 and 400,000 years ago and that may be a direct ancestor of both *Homo neanderthalensis* in Europe and *Homo sapiens*. These hominins used a stone tool technology similar to Acheulean. Many paleoanthropologists see this as a synonym for "archaic *Homo sapiens*."

Piltdown Man: a "discovery" in 1912 in England that was believed to be the "missing link" between apes and humans by the majority of the scientific community. In 1953, it was proven to be a hoax.

preneandertal hypothesis: hypothesis that a preneandertal hominin was the direct ancestor of both Neandertals and *Homo sapiens*, diverging about 200,000 years ago.

presapiens hypothesis: hypothesis that Neandertals and *Homo sapiens* had separate lineages long before 200,000 years ago.

Suggested Reading

Stringer, *Homo britannicus*.

Questions to Consider

1. How might this debate have been different if Neandertals had been found only in some other part of the world instead of Europe?

2. The Neandertal genome has made the identity of Middle Pleistocene Europeans very intriguing. How might we explain the apparently very recent relationship of Neandertals and Africans?

What Do Stone Tools Reveal about Early Man?
Lecture 14

Early archaeologists systematized the stone tool traditions in prehistory by recognizing types of artifacts that might be found in one tradition and not in others. The French archaeologist François Bordes interpreted similar archaeological assemblages as representatives of a single cultural group. This interpretation was challenged by the American archaeologist Lewis Binford, who reasoned that differences between stone tool assemblages reflected the different kinds of activities that might have been done at an ephemeral site. This debate hasn't been settled, but it has deepened our understanding of ancient sites.

Roc de Marsal is a cave outside of Les Eyzies in France. In this cave was a very dense strata of stone tools, animal bones that Neandertals were hunting, and ash from their fires. At the base of the cave, Jean Lafille found the skeleton of a 3-year-old child, one of the earliest known burials in the human paleontological record. This site is the capital of prehistory because of the number of Paleolithic sites that are around it. Especially in the 1970s, there has been a focused debate about the nature of interpretation of archaeological remains.

This debate was most notably between 2 of the giant figures in the field: François Bordes, the mature French prehistorian, and Lewis Binford, the young American. Bordes interpreted stone tools as evidence of different ancient cultures that left different kinds of stone tools. On the other hand, Binford argued that these different stone tool assemblages were left by people who were doing different activities, so the stone tools were information about why and how people were using sites—not necessarily about culture.

The Bordes-Binford debate is really about the type of the Middle Paleolithic found in France and Europe broadly called the Mousterian, the stone tool industry made by most Neandertals. It's not just a Neandertal industry; some of the early modern humans found in West Asia and North Africa were Mousterian people. This tool industry is not only spread over a broad space, but it's also spread over a relatively broad time.

When we look at Mousterian tool assemblages, the initial definition was from a site called Le Moustier, from which "Mousterian" gets its name, in France. These stone tool artifacts were initially made by Neandertals that were living there 50,000 years ago, but now we find this style of tools in many places. A Mousterian tool is one that has a large frequency of points, such as spears and scrapers.

François Bordes analyzed the topic of what makes different assemblages of Mousterian tools different from each other in a very unique way. He studied assemblages of tools by plotting how many tools of each type he found at a site; this data formed a curve that represented the types and proportions of artifacts he found. The shape of the curve allowed him to compare different assemblages with each other in terms of the representation of tools.

Sometimes archaeologists find a mix of different tool types with similar technology at sites. For instance, if you find a predominantly Mousterian site with hand axes mixed in, you might determine that it evolved from an early stone industry, Acheulean, to a slightly more sophisticated Mousterian industry with Acheulean influences. A site like this became called a Mousterian of Acheulean tradition, or MTA.

Bordes had to explain why different types of tools were separated into different levels at some sites. He reasoned that these were different groups that had interacted and had occupied these sites at different times and that this was a record of all the people who had lived there and their cultures.

From the standpoint of developing our technology, a unique form of tool manufacture that Neandertals used is called the Levallois technique, which involves the use of a core, a piece of rock, and the removal of flakes from that rock to make a standardized shape. It is used to produce what is called a Levallois flake, which is easily recognizable because it has scars on one side and it is smooth on the other.

Bordes noticed that these artifacts were different in frequency in different Mousterian assemblages but could not determine the reasoning behind this. Instead, this topic was taken up by the man who became Bordes's debate partner, Lewis Binford, who tried to determine how to invoke within the archaeological record a scene of the anthropology of the people as they interacted with artifacts.

It was Binford's goal to integrate the different activities that might've occurred for short or long periods of time and separate them to discover what kinds of activities were going on. He called his study of the archaeological record middle-range theory; the idea was to find out what lay in between the artifacts and the people who had made them. Binford looked at Bordes's records and evaluated which tools are found in conjunction with each other. For example, when he found an abundance of scrapers with points, he reasoned that these were likely places where men were hunting and working directly with the animals' carcasses.

The debate between Bordes and Binford was hugely formative to the way that archaeologists think about the archaeological record. Over the course of the subsequent 40 years, archaeologists have become more sophisticated. In a process called zooarchaeology, archaeologists study the bones from animals that are left by the hunters. One way of using zooarchaeology is to determine the ages of the animals that are being hunted.

Archaeologists can also examine the process of tool manufacture and think about the different ways that tools are related to other tools. Harold Dibble had the idea that when you looked at a Mousterian assemblage, many of the different artifact types are actually the same artifact in different stages of its lifespan—people use a tool, it gets worn out, and it needs to be sharpened, which transforms it into a different artifact within Bordes' classification. In this kind of analysis, called reduction sequence analysis, it's the initial starting point that affects how the finished tool ends up.

Modern archaeologists have come to a view that's similar to Bordes's view. We are able to look at the cultures of people that existed, but we do so by taking a very skeptical view of the science, as Binford did. The lesson in the debate between Bordes and Binford is that archaeologists sharpened their arguments through this interaction, and it led to more developments within the science and a greater sophistication of our understanding of Neandertal behavior. ■

Suggested Reading

Binford, *In Pursuit of the Past*.

Questions to Consider

1. We share some technologies very rapidly today, but sometimes cultures remain very distinct in their tools—like forks versus chopsticks. What kinds of artifacts today make reliable markers of culture?

2. Binford's arguments were based on observing hunting and gathering societies, which are rapidly disappearing. Are there other analogs for ancient behavior that simply no longer exist?

Did Neandertals Speak?
Lecture 15

Language is a defining characteristic of humanity today. But we don't know when and where it arose. The main organs supporting language—the brain and vocal apparatus—do not fossilize. Many scientists have claimed that language is a modern human trait, giving us the edge over archaic humans who lacked speech. Others have recognized humanlike cultural sophistication in Neandertals and argue that they must have had language, possibly in the fully human sense.

Paleoanthropologists are often in a position where they would very much like to be able to study the origin of some kind of human characteristic, but the fossil record just doesn't cooperate. There is no human characteristic that is as central to our understanding of how humans interact with each other as language, but before the invention of writing, we can't tell anything about what people might have talked to each other about.

We want to understand the origin of language, but when we look at the skeleton, there is almost no sign of any of the structures that are related to language in what we can see externally. Even though Neandertals lived a relatively short time ago, there is a gulf between us in terms of the record that they left and what we know that living people are capable of. Is that gulf explained by the interactions those people had with each other?

Up until the very recent past, studying skeletons was the only way to study language.

Up until the very recent past, studying skeletons was the only way to study language. Philip Lieberman looked at fossil crania and tried to interpret the angulation of the base of the skull in terms of how it would relate to the anatomy of the throat. Lieberman believed that the shallow-angled skulls of Neandertals created apelike speech patterns—not human language.

The throat is not the ideal source of evidence about language because the vocalization part is not necessarily the most essential element—it's the brain. However, interpreting the structure of the brain is very difficult. Ralph Holloway, while studying the ER 1470 skull, noticed that Broca's area was more prominent on the left side, which was a hint that language ability might have been changing as early as *Homo habilis*. This is really the only hint that we have from the brain in terms of anatomy.

Today, we can learn quite a bit about the structure of speech in the brain by studying the genes that are involved in brain development. The most important of those genes is called the **FoxP2 gene**, which binds to DNA and helps regulate the action of other genes during the development of the speech areas of the left side of the brain. We know this gene is connected to speech because of its influence in rare living people who have a mutated version of it.

Humans have 2 changes in this gene that aren't present in any other kinds of mammals—not in chimpanzees or in other primates. It turns out that these same 2 changes are also present in the genomes of Neandertals, which is a hint in favor of the idea that whatever changes humans have that start to underlie language are changes that Neandertals share with us.

In the last several years, looking at the speech apparatus and the hearing apparatus has really taken strides because of developments in the fossil record and in our technology. A tiny bone in the throat called the **hyoid bone** floats in the tissues of your throat and supports the ligaments that keep your larynx in the right place. Because it's so small and is not normally connected to the rest of the skeleton, it is incredibly rare to find in any kind of fossil context.

In recent years, however, several hyoid bones have been recovered from fossil hominins of different kinds. One of these comes from a child skeleton of *Australopithecus afarensis* found at a site in Ethiopia called Dikika. This child had a well-preserved hyoid bone in the throat that was unlike those found in recent people. Instead, the throat of *afarensis* appears to have been adapted to make vocalizations that were chimpanzee-like.

Later in the fossil record, we also have some hyoid bones. We have found 3 hyoid bones that come from our genus, *Homo*, that contrast with the anatomy of the hyoid bone in the Dikika skeleton. Unlike that earlier australopithecine skeleton, these human skeletons have a very simplified hyoid bone with a humanlike anatomy. This finding supplements the one hyoid bone that we had in the fossil record, up until 10 years ago, that came from a Neandertal that lived in Israel about 50,000 to 60,000 years ago. That hyoid bone came from a skeleton at a site called Kebara and was also humanlike in its anatomy.

The other aspect of the vocal auditory channel—the channel that we use for speaking and listening—is the ear, and studying ears in the fossil record is not simple either. The structures in the ear that are relevant for language are structures that lie inside of the temporal bone in a part that anatomists called the **petrous portion** of the temporal bone. The petrous portion is one of the hardest bones in the body, and you have to get inside it to study the tiny bones of the ear, which hasn't been done with fossils until very recently. Now we can scan inside the temporal bone using micro CT scanners, and we can reconstruct the shape of the middle ear bones.

When we study the middle ear bones of the Atapuerca fossils—those fossils from Spain that are 600,000 years old—we can produce a computer model of the morphology of these bones that can help us determine what kinds of sounds will be transmitted effectively by the bones. In contrast to chimpanzee-like middle ear bones, the Atapuerca middle ear bones are better able to conduct middle frequency sounds, which are the frequencies that humans can hear better than chimpanzees and that humans use to differentiate speech sounds from each other. This is evidence in favor of the idea that both speech and hearing evolved together, and we have genetic evidence of this as well.

As a result of studying deafness in humans, we understand a lot about the genetics of the hair cells in the inner ear. **Alpha-tectorin**, an intimate structure involved in these hair cells, is a gene that appears to have been evolving rapidly in our evolution, based on the fact that it has 17 changes between chimpanzees and humans. Neandertals have the human version of this gene with just one exception, so most of the changes in this system were occurring earlier in our evolution than our divergence from Neandertals.

Present evidence points in favor of Neandertals (and probably other kinds of early humans) having speech. It is not clear whether their language would have been different from ours in some systematic way, or what that different (presumably simpler) kind of language would look like. But the cultural and anatomical evidence points toward a significant and important language ability in Neandertals, even if it were not identical to our own. ■

Important Terms

alpha-tectorin: protein found in the inner ear, as part of a structure called the tectorial membrane, which helps to convert sound waves to nerve impulses—a critical process for hearing.

FoxP2 gene: a gene involved in early brain development. The normal form of this gene in humans appears to be important for language development.

hyoid bone: horseshoe-shaped bone situated in the neck that serves as an anchoring structure for the larynx. It is critical for speech production.

petrous portion: a pyramid-shaped part of the temporal bone that encloses the middle and inner ear. It is one of the hardest parts of the skeleton.

Suggested Reading

Trinkaus and Shipman, *The Neanderthals*.

Questions to Consider

1. We think of Stone Age technology as being relatively simple, but how much would be possible without any kind of language at all?

2. We use the vocal system to communicate tones and sounds that are not themselves parts of language. How might these nonverbal forms of communication have been different in early hominins who had different vocal or auditory systems than ours?

Neandertals—Extinct or Ancestors?
Lecture 16

Anthropologists argued about whether Neandertals could have been our ancestors for a very long time. Many believed they were too different or too specialized to be part of our species. Others have minimized the differences. Some have even found significant similarities between Neandertals and later people in Europe suggesting that they mated and had offspring.

The Neandertals were the first example where people were able to look into the fossil record and determine that they don't exist anymore, but they are related to us. Are we their descendents, or are they extinct? This has been a basic debate since the very beginnings of paleoanthropology. Today, we have more evidence about them than we have about any other kind of ancient archaic human, and yet this question remains.

Neandertals existed in Europe from around 200,000 years ago up to about 30,000 years ago. In the context of our evolution, this is the last kind of archaic human to exist before the appearance of more modern-looking people throughout the world. That time period is a period of really rapid change, in climate terms and in human biological terms.

Neandertals existed in Europe from around 200,000 years ago up to about 30,000 years ago.

Neandertals are a sample of ancient humans for which we have vastly more specimens than for any other population of ancient people. Because of sites like Krapina in Croatia, we understand a lot about the anatomy and variation in the Neandertal population. We also have a number of relatively complete skeletons because Neandertals did something that earlier humans had never done—they buried their dead.

When we look at the crania of these skeletons, we find that their skulls have a number of features that are distinct compared to living humans. If we look at a Neandertal skull from the top, it has sort of a teardrop shape, but the modern human skull is wider toward the top. In addition, their **mastoid processes**, the bony processes right behind the ear, were short, which indicates a difference in the attachment of the muscles of the neck to the base of the skull.

Overall, the bones of the legs and arms of Neandertals are thick. This tells us that they were putting a lot of force through those bones. Their activity level was very high, but the fact that their legs are relatively short is indicative of an adaptation to cold. Europe was the coldest place at the time that humans were living, so Neandertals were adapting to this climate by changing their body proportions.

If humans today lack these specializations that Neandertals were using either to adapt themselves to the cold or to their activity pattern, then that's a fairly compelling argument that we don't have a lot of genetic input from them. The first person who set out the idea that Neandertals are quite different from us in an evolutionary sense was Ernst Haeckel.

In addition to Haeckel, German theorist Gustav Schwalbe examined the possible relations of Neandertals with us. He laid out 2 schemes—a scheme in which the Neandertals were our ancestors and a scheme in which the Neandertals had branched off from us and had their own evolutionary trajectory. This formed the basis for later systematic comparisons of anatomy in Neandertal specimens.

At Mladeč, in the Czech Republic, there's a series of fossils that were unearthed in the early 20th century that date to over 30,000 years ago. Just as the Peking Man fossils had been lost during WWII, the Mladeč fossils were among the pillaged pieces of cultural artifacts that the Nazis took from across central Europe. However, we have descriptions of these fossils along with some surviving specimens. Anthropologists determined that some of the specimens had Neandertal-looking characteristics, and it was Dave Frayer's argument that this sample reflected genetic input from Neandertals.

Today we have a much more direct source of evidence about Neandertal relationships with us; we have genetic material from them. To extract genes from ancient European fossils, bone powder is extracted from the fossils because it preserves the organic material—it contains DNA. With the right chemical steps, and with the right kind of purification, you can reconstruct parts of that DNA.

The **mitochondrial DNA** is a special part that exists outside of the nucleus of each cell and has its own little loop of DNA. It's very tiny compared to what most of your genome is, but that tiny loop mutates more quickly than most of our DNA and is genealogically unique. Because of this, it is much more distinctive, and it can reflect some evolutionary events fairly quickly.

By comparing the mitochondrial DNA of humans and Neandertals, we found that there were many differences: All living people today share one basic type of mitochondria compared to Neandertals, and all of the Neandertals that we have sampled share a different type. Based on the molecular clock, it appears that Neandertals and humans diverged from each other sometime before 400,000 years ago.

If Neandertals had survived, we would expect that their DNA would survive at least in some small fraction. In fact, after sampling thousands of living people, nobody was found with this Neandertal type of mitochondrial DNA. This method seems to provide really convincing evidence that the Neandertals were extinct, and it is a good way to identify whether fossils are Neandertal based on whether they have this type of DNA.

Another way to consider the skeletal evidence of Neandertals is to examine the complete nuclear genome. Different genes have different functions, and when populations mix with each other, they don't necessarily inherit all of the genes that would've come from both of the ancestors—it isn't a perfect blending of the 2. This situation occurs in nature quite frequently.

In 2010, Tim White found a sample of the rest of the Neandertals genome from a little piece of a shinbone discovered at a site called Vindija in Croatia. DNA extraction from this bone turned out to be the most successful DNA extraction from any of the Neandertals that had ever been attempted.

The way we can reconstruct a genome today is by sequencing every little piece of DNA and then using computers to figure out their location on the genetic map. With the genetic map, we're able to reconstruct a genome by building it out of these tiny parts. We're also able to sort out elements that are similar to the human genome from the ones that aren't. This process is an amazing technological feat.

Analysis of the Neandertal genome indicates that it contributed around 3% of the DNA of people outside Africa today. Neandertals were not the predominant part of our ancestry, but they contributed some pieces. The Denisova genome is not a major contributor to most populations, except for today's population of Sahul—New Guinea, Australia, and Melanesia. The regional differences are very striking and may indicate the history of dispersal from Africa and mixture as people passed through West and South Asia to their present locations. ■

Important Terms

mastoid process: the bony process behind the ear to which several muscles attach. It is typically smaller in Neandertals than in modern humans.

mitochondrial DNA: the DNA found in organelles called mitochondria that is located outside of the cell nucleus and is inherited only from the mother. Mitochondrial DNA is a powerful tool for tracking ancestry through females and has been used in this role to track human ancestry back hundreds of generations. It includes only around 16,000 base pairs as opposed to the 3 billion in a copy of the nuclear genome.

Suggested Reading

Hawks, John. *John Hawks Weblog*.

Questions to Consider

1. How should we feel about having Neandertal ancestors? Does it matter that some people living today have much less Neandertal ancestry than others and that some have none?

2. Neandertals seem to have lived in very small populations with many fewer people than lived in Africa at the same time. Why?

Is Our Neandertal Heritage Important?
Lecture 17

Neandertals are gone, but some of their genes still persist in some human populations, especially outside of Africa. As markers of ancestry, these genes may tell us about the history and interactions of modern humans with archaic humans, but they may not relate to any behaviors or functions that have any visibly important effects. In other parts of the world, we don't yet know whether archaic people contributed genes to recent populations, but a few skeletal traits suggest that such contributions might have happened, and geneticists have begun to uncover DNA evidence from these hominins.

Are the genes that we inherited from Neandertals useful or just random? Over the last 150 years, a debate existed about whether Neandertals were our ancestors at all. Even scientists who accepted that we might have some ancestry from this ancient group of people disagreed on the importance of what we received from this ancestry. We know that we have common ancestors with Neandertals, but in addition to that, we know that we have Neandertal ancestors because of evidence from our genetic makeup.

The one gene we know the most about in Neandertals is the mitochondrial DNA, which is inherited only along the maternal line, or from the mother to the offspring. This unique form of inheritance means that we can trace the ancestry of mitochondrial DNA with some great accuracy because the DNA doesn't recombine generation to generation, scrambling up its order and thereby confusing our study of its genealogy.

We have more than a dozen Neandertals from whom we've got complete mitochondrial DNA sequences, which tell us that the Neandertal mitochondrial DNA was very limited in variation; it came from a relatively small number of ancestors within the last 150,000 years. However, Neandertal mitochondrial sequences are all distinct from ours, so we have to evaluate the Neandertal contribution to our DNA by looking at other parts of the genome—the nuclear genome.

A specimen found in the Denisova Cave in Siberia has a mitochondrial DNA that is distinct from both humans and Neandertals. However, the nuclear genome of this specimen is much more similar to Neandertals than the mitochondrial DNA is. This mismatch tells us that the mitochondrial DNA followed a different kind of history than most of the genome—it must have been affected in its evolution by its function through natural selection.

Caves around the world contain some of the richest samples of hominin skulls.

When we compare the actual gene sequence of the mitochondrial DNA, it looks like the mitochondria of Neandertals may have been adapted to a different energy environment than the mitochondria of living people. This is not surprising if we consider Neandertals living in a cold environment without the technology to make appropriate clothing. Perhaps the evolution of the mitochondria is the reason Neandertals no longer exist.

Using today's gene-mapping technology, if we were to map the mitochondrial DNA of Neandertals to show where in the world people live who have similar mitochondria, the map would be blank. The other major marker, the Y chromosome, is also a dead end because the Neandertals that we have genome sequences for are all females, who don't have Y chromosomes. Our 2 big pieces of genealogical information are missing, so we need to look at genealogy in a somewhat different way.

Today, we are examining the genealogy of different parts of the genome and trying to connect people with each other to see when the ancestors of different parts of their genome lived, and also trying to connect them to these archaic hominids. This is an ongoing study in which we try to determine which parts of the human genome are derived from Neandertals and which parts have no sign of Neandertal contribution.

If you analyze your complete genome using a sample of genotypes, you'll get a broad sense of where your ancestors lived by comparing different segments of your genome to other people in different parts of the world. What you might discover is that some segments of the genome have a copy that is very common in a particular place.

If we only had genes that we share with Neandertals because we have a distant ancestor in common with Neandertals, then everybody living today would be equally like or unlike the Neandertals. However, when we compare these 2 genomes, we find that people today who live outside of Africa have more Neandertal in them. This is geographically consistent with the idea that Neandertals who lived outside of Africa were interacting with people and contributed some of their genes to those people. What this doesn't tell us, though, is which parts of the genome are especially Neandertal-like and which parts of the genome aren't.

A specimen found in the Denisova Cave in Siberia has a mitochondrial DNA that is distinct from both humans and Neandertals.

There are some pretty clear cases where humans and Neandertals are similar to each other and where the Denisova genome is different from both of us. One of those areas is a part of the genome called HAR1, which stands for the human accelerated region. We find that the evolution of this part of the genome was going on during the time that humans, Neandertals, and Denisovans were differentiating from each other.

In order to talk about the things that all of us have in common, we can look at many aspects of the human genome that Neandertals lack, and the mitochondrial DNA is one of them. In fact, there are several parts of the genome in which humans sampled today have one kind of sequence while Neandertals have a different kind of sequence. In these cases, Neandertal cells are operating in a slightly different way from human cells. When we examine a broad sample of people, we discover that these differences emerged during our evolution.

Finding the genes that we inherited directly from Neandertals is a real challenge. A significant thing we've learned about Neandertal genes in human populations now is that different populations of people outside of Africa, for example, Europeans and Chinese people, have different Neandertal genes, although there's some overlap. It seems that when the mixture took place between humans and Neandertals, it was before a time when human populations began to separate and become isolated from one another.

We're beginning to understand the paleobiology that gave rise to our current distribution of Neandertal genes. Although we have found some differences between the genomes of humans and Neandertals, it's not yet clear whether these differences have any effect on phenotype, which is the anatomical or behavioral makeup. In order to examine genome differences on a phenotypical level, we're going to have to compare how different people with different copies of these genes actually map out. This part of paleoanthropology is a science that is building rapidly, and it's likely that we'll have many answers to this within the next few years. ■

Questions to Consider

1. The features we are most likely to recognize as different in Neandertals are the skeletal and dental features that are uncommon or absent from today's people. Are there less-visible parts of our biology that we might share more with these ancient humans?

2. The archaic genomes help to show us that different genes in humans have different histories. How do gene histories compare to genealogical histories?

Multiregional Evolution versus Out of Africa
Lecture 18

Some anthropologists long argued for a single origin of humanity. Because humans today share many features not found in fossil people, the origin might be quite recent, within the last 100,000 years or so. The maximum variability in humans is within Africa today, so the single origin location would be most likely Africa—hence the "out of Africa" hypothesis. Others argued that today's people share similarities with ancient humans in the same region of the world. The multiregional evolution hypothesis explains this continuity by partial ancestry.

During the 1940s, people debated whether humans derived from one population that spread from West Asia, or whether instead the evolution of people had been drawn from many regions with mixture. This debate is the debate between the **multiregional hypothesis** and the **out of Africa hypothesis**. Although this debate has a historical background, it has been mostly settled in recent years.

The multiregional hypothesis states that humans today originated in different populations that lived in different parts of the world in the past—that there was a multiregional contribution to our ancestry as living people that gave rise to our current diversity. On the other hand, the out of Africa hypothesis states that today's population derived from a small population that lived in Africa and dispersed throughout the rest of the world.

It was as people started to put together the fossil record into a worldwide picture that these 2 hypotheses originated. The first person who thought about the evolution of humans in a multiregional sense was Franz Weidenreich, who discovered the Peking Man. He was impressed at the degree to which these Chinese fossils showed similar kinds of characteristics to the fossils from Java. He was also struck by the fact that the regional differences between these 2 were similar in pattern to the kinds of differences that occur between people in different populations today, thinking about it in terms of different races. These ideas formed the basis for his **polycentric hypothesis**, which states that modern humans came into existence by the interaction of several ancient centers of evolution.

At around the same time, anthropologist William W. Howells was also trying to systematize the fossil record, but he had a very different point of view. He looked at the skeletal variation in living people throughout the world and noticed that living people are much more similar to each other than they are to any of the people that we have as fossils, which tells us that they probably had a common origin that they don't share with these other ancient fossil people.

At that time, the best known samples of fossil humans of around the right antiquity to be ancestors of modern humans came from Mount Carmel in Israel. These skeletons looked like they had a mixture of Neandertal and human characteristics. Because of this sample, Howells determined that the origin of living people could be found in a population like this one. This was the first real conception that there was a central source for humanity and that we should be looking for our commonalities with rather than our differences from the known fossil varieties of humans.

Interestingly, early and later fossils found in Java do not share many similar features with people who currently live in Java.

When Weidenreich looked at the fossil record of Java, he looked for features that were similar to other more recent people living in the same part of the world, and he found many of them. He looked at some later specimens from Java and determined that they, too, shared similar kinds of characteristics. However, living people in Java did not look like these fossils; they had much more rounded skulls.

Weidenreich tried to remedy this situation by comparing the skeletal remains of Australian aboriginal people with these ancient Javan people. In doing so, he determined that one of the genealogical ties in Australians' ancestry must have come from Java; an evolution must have occurred that involved the movement of people between populations.

After Weidenreich's death, the multiregional idea was developed by Milford Wolpoff and others as a description of populations connected by genetic exchanges. In this view, genes from one population would flow to another under selection so that the adaptive traits would spread throughout the world and the traits that made regions relatively more distinctive were probably not adapted.

Genetic evidence appeared to favor the out of Africa hypothesis because human **genetic variation**, differences in genes caused by mutation, is low. Researchers sampled DNA from people around the world and discovered that the DNA was very similar, just as Howells had observed that the anatomy of people in the world today is more similar to each other than to fossils in the past. If this genetic variation were determined by a small population size, it would mean that humans had been limited to a small size within the last 200,000 years.

In general, the multiregional hypothesis is correct.

The Neandertal and Denisova genomes show that the population size explanation is not sufficient because some genes are shared outside of Africa with these archaic genomes. The Neandertal genome shows that there was a population in Africa that did expand and did spread its genes throughout the world, but that when it got there it mixed with the people who were already there. This theory has been confirmed by the Denisova DNA genome because this specimen isn't a Neandertal, but its genome shares similarities with some living people.

In general, the multiregional hypothesis is correct. It appears that there was a population that existed in the west of Eurasia, Neandertals, that mixed with emerging Africans in West Asia. There was also a population that existed in the East, represented by the Denisova specimen, that was spread across Southeast Asia that people mixed with as they went along the southern boundary of those areas to their easternmost extreme.

In addition, most of our genome does reflect an African origin; we must look into African populations to understand how today's diversity has come about. Today, the diversity that exists outside of Africa is only a fragment of the diversity that currently exists inside of Africa—a fragment that reflects only a portion of our overall diversity as a species. ■

Important Terms

genetic variation: differences in genes brought about by mutation, providing the "raw material" for natural selection.

multiregional hypothesis: the hypothesis that modern humans evolved from a population of archaic humans (including Neandertals and *Homo erectus*) that was spread across much of the Old World by a process of selection and genetic exchange.

out of Africa hypothesis: hypothesis that all modern humans stem from a single group of *Homo sapiens* who emigrated from Africa within the last 100,000 years, mostly replacing other early humans (such as Neandertals) rather than interbreeding with them.

polycentric hypothesis: the name for Franz Weidenreich's hypothesis that modern humans came into existence by the interaction of several ancient centers of evolution—chiefly Africa, Asia, and Europe.

Suggested Reading

Stringer and McKie, *African Exodus*.

Wolpoff and Caspari, *Race and Human Evolution*.

Questions to Consider

1. What reasons might explain why the evolution of modern humans seems tied to a massive migration and turnover of ancient people outside Africa?

2. Weidenreich and Howells debated basically the same issues that became important during the 1980s and 1990s. Why did this question have such resonance for paleoanthropologists?

Climate's Impact on Our Evolution
Lecture 19

Several lines of evidence point to the idea that our ancestors had a very small population size at some point in the last 100,000 years—what has been called a "bottleneck." Geologist Michael Rampino, archaeologist Stanley Ambrose, and others have suggested that the bottleneck might have been driven by the Toba volcanic eruption, the largest catastrophic event of the Pleistocene, which altered the Earth's climate around 74,000 years ago. However, this hypothesis has several weaknesses that are noted by critics.

A volcano on the island of Sumatra called Mt. Toba erupted 74,000 years ago. This was the largest volcanic eruption that occurred at any time during human evolution, and it probably had catastrophic effects on the earth's climate. It probably cooled the earth substantially, and some geologists suspect that it had a catastrophic effect on human populations by eliminating those who could not survive in this new climate. It is also possible that this event was involved with the origin of modern humans and their diversification in the world after the eruption.

The way that we address climate hypotheses has to do both with our understanding of human biology and with our understanding of the earth's environment. As we saw in the last lecture, modern humans trace most of the genetic material today back to Africa, and our genetic heritage is therefore a question of the population interactions that were occurring within Africa during the past few hundred thousand years.

We have found that the genetic diversity that exists in Africa reflects the diversity that once was more expansive across Africa. When we look into the more distant past, it's our goal to try to connect the genealogies of people so that we can trace their ancestors back into more ancient populations.

When we look into the distant past for humans, the population size aspect of our genetic variation becomes dominant. The more you go back into the past, the more likely it is that 2 genes will share an ancestor. But, if we look at any particular generation in the past, it is very much like a decay function—there's a high likelihood now, but it shrinks with every generation that we go back. From this relationship, we can estimate the size of ancient populations.

In the scope of hundreds of thousands of years, we estimate that the size of the ancient human population was—not a billion individuals, not even of a million individuals—about 10,000 individuals. That's a lot smaller than the human population now, and it raises an immediate question in a hypothesis. Are we looking at the actual size of the human population, and if so, was this a **population bottleneck**—a time when humans crashed down to a small population size, existed for some time, and then later started to grow so that we have today's very large human population? This logic was really key to developing the out of Africa hypothesis.

Why is it that humans today have low genetic variability?

Why is it that humans today have low genetic variability? The answer, with respect to other primates, is because our populations were more inbred. We're inbred as a species because the lines of our genealogy go back so fast that it's simply impossible that they can't trace back to the same number of people. We have more ancestors tracing back to a smaller number of people, and that kind of relationship has been important in understanding the dispersal of people through the world and the growth of the human population.

From the standpoint of the origination of modern humans, the small population size is a mystery. One clear hypothesis is climate. There have been intense climate changes in Africa, Europe, and Asia in the past, and humans had to endure those changes. Maybe humans didn't endure them very well and were constrained to a small population size.

The study of ancient climate is done with ice cores and with other kinds of deep cores; they provide ways of studying how things have changed in particular places in the past. From these sources of evidence, we've gained a pretty clear understanding of the way that earth's climate has fluctuated over the course of the last million years or more. During this time, there have been several distinct glacial cycles that were driven by changes in the amount of sunlight that the earth received because of changes in the shape of the Earth's orbit, which creates the opportunity for glaciers to advance and recede.

The 4 climate cycles that the earth has gone through in the last million years have been hugely important in the way that we understand the physiography of the kinds of rock and sediments we find in the northern continents, but also in terms of how we expect people were able to move. It is clear that when glaciers recede, people expand to other areas in response. What's less clear is the extent to which large earlier climate shocks, like the Toba eruption, might've affected people.

When we look at the Toba eruption and compare it with the climate records that we find in ice cores, we discover that the eruption coincides with the time of greatest intensification of the Würm glaciation, the last major Ice Age, which probably did have catastrophic impacts on human populations. The question that remains is whether the Toba eruption restricted the size of the human population at the time.

Archaeologically, we know that the Neandertals moved out of northern Europe whenever the glaciers advanced, so we can say that there is a direct relationship of climate on their distribution. But, when we look at the Neandertals as a population, it's very clear that this eruption didn't annihilate them or their genetic diversity. This particular event did not reduce us to a small population; it had to have been something that had occurred further back in time that could have influenced both our variation and the Neandertal variation that many of us carry.

We can also address the question of the Toba eruption by looking at particular archaeological sites that are within the fallout zone of the eruption. One of these is in India at a site called Jwalapuram, which has been dug by Mike Petraglia of Oxford University. His excavations have shown that there's a distinct level that corresponds to the Toba ash layer and that there are stone tools under and above this layer, which shows that the population persisted without a large impact from the Toba eruption.

Even though the Toba eruption did not cause the human population to be reduced to a small number because humans were able to adapt to the change in climate, it still had important effects on the Earth's climate, possibly triggering the onset of one of the major phases of the last ice age. The importance of these climate factors in our evolution is a major topic of investigation today. ■

Important Term

population bottleneck: an evolutionary event in which a population is limited to a very small number of individuals for a significant time. A bottleneck can cause inbreeding in a population and may be an explanation for why human mitochondrial variation is very limited.

Suggested Reading

Olson, *Mapping Human History*.

Relethford, *Reflections of Our Past*.

Questions to Consider

1. Some anthropologists see ancient catastrophes as evidence of human adaptability; others see them as warnings about the chance survival and extinction of populations. What can these ancient events tell us about ourselves?

2. Why has genetic variation been so difficult to apply to understanding ancient population size?

Language—Adaptation or Spandrel?
Lecture 20

> Language is the basis of much human behavior but has no clear antecedent among our primate relatives. An influential school of linguists, led by Noam Chomsky, argue that our minds have a fixed and innate ability to learn language in a way that develops differently in different languages. They suggest that the biology of language may have evolved for another purpose related to thought or cognition, and only later for communication. Developmental psychologists challenge that hypothesis, arguing that the fundamental cognitive abilities underlying language are not specific to language at all.

Language is such an important aspect of human behavior, and it's something that is pretty novel in our evolution. There are no other species that communicate the way that we do, so it's a big mystery in our evolution how language emerged. In the context of psychology and biology, the subject of how language evolved has been a long-running debate.

In this debate, there are 2 camps: one sees language itself as the primary target of natural selection in the emergence of the human brain, and the other sees language as a side effect of the evolution of other kinds of cognitive skills in humans. We have to look beyond the fossil record to try to determine how language evolved.

In the context of psychology and biology, the subject of how language evolved has been a long-running debate.

Language is a very distinct form of communication because unlike visual communication, which is multimodal, language is a form of communication that is serial—it has to follow an order because people make sounds using their vocal tract, throat, and mouth. Those sounds are transmitted to a listener, who will hear those sounds with their ears. That channel means that language has to be structured in a very special way.

In the fossil record, we have very little evidence about the structure of the brain and, in particular, the structure of the brain areas that may be related to language. In order to learn about this level of structuring of language, we have to depend on what we can understand from human development, from the way other kinds of animals naturally communicate, and from the ways they can be trained to replicate some kinds of human communication.

Because chimpanzees and bonobos don't have the vocal channel that we do, they can't produce human speech sounds, but they can learn how to sign. Kanzi, who we studied in terms of tool manufacture, mastered a series of hundreds of logograms and has taught them to others. However, Kanzi has never mastered the combination of signs into longer utterances, something humans can manage by age 2 or 3. Compared to humans, there seems to be a difference in chimpanzees' ability to generate this higher level of structure known as grammar.

Grammar has been the central focus of linguistics since the beginning. The most famous figure in the study of grammar is a linguist named Noam Chomsky, who made an innatist argument in the context of language: He argued that there are patterns that occur in human languages that cannot be learned by simply listening to what other people say. Humans seem to be born with an innate ability to sift out patterns that aren't obvious from the speech around them so they can create those patterns. Chomsky calls this argument the poverty of the stimulus—the stimuli that are present in an environment aren't enough to master a natural language.

Chomsky generalized his argument to say that if we have the ability to make an infinitely complicated series of linguistic utterances by adding repetitive elements—the recursive ability of language—how does natural selection account for that ability? Natural selection can only operate on what actually occurs in the population, but language is so much more in its potential than has ever occurred in any population.

Chomsky explains natural selection's effect on language by arguing that the complicated abilities that we have may be side effects of our evolution of other kinds of cognitive behaviors, and language might've emerged when the brain got to be complicated enough that it was able to generalize social and manipulative behaviors into communication.

Evolutionary biologist Stephen Jay Gould collaborated with geneticist Richard Lewontin to give us a way of talking about the adaptation of abilities as a side effect of other kinds of evolutionary constraints. To do this, they used a cathedral as an example. Most cathedrals with a dome have arches to support it that are architecturally very strong. A dome that sits on top of a series of arches will have triangular spaces, called **spandrels**, in between the arches that support the dome.

Spandrels are an architectural necessity, but in many cathedrals, the spandrels are elaborately decorated and become important in the life of the religious community that worships inside the church. If you ask a patron of the church about the purpose of the spandrels, he or she will tell you about the religious scenes that are depicted on the spandrels. But that is not the purpose of the spandrels—they are there to hold up the dome.

Gould took Chomsky's ideas and said maybe language is there because of the adaptation of other cognitive abilities, but those cognitive abilities that evolve for other purposes were built upon for communication purposes so that the cognitive complexity of humans underlies language and the particular elaboration of language might itself be innate because of these other things.

Gould's view of language was met with opposition on the part of some linguists and biologists. One of these was Steven Pinker, a follower of Chomsky, who also believed that our ability to learn language is basically innate and that genes or working with our environment enable us to develop as speaking adults. However, Pinker thought that this could be a straightforward product of natural selection—that it can't just be a side effect of other cognitive abilities. He believed that learning language is largely an instinctive process.

Today's linguists disagree with Pinker and Chomsky about the extent to which language is innate. Many believe that language is largely learned uniquely and differently by different kinds of people. One argument in favor of this idea is brain **plasticity**. In cases where a person has had his or her brain's left hemisphere removed because of a severe kind of seizure disorder, sometimes they are able to instantiate language on the opposite side of their brain.

Probably the biggest figure today in favor of the point of view that language is largely shared and learned rather than being mainly innate is Michael Tomasello, who believes that language is built using cultural processes more than genes. In his studies, he has found that there seems to be an aspect of learning that has relatively little to do with communication but has a lot to do with the ability to focus on the same object and get that same object in an attention span between 2 individuals. This is a skill that's fundamental to language in humans, but it seems to have emerged some time during our evolution, and it seems to be a uniquely human aspect of behavior.

Did language emerge as a product of selection—as a target of adaptation in our evolution—or did language emerge as a side effect of selection on other processes—as a spandrel? There is still an active debate about the extent to which natural selection was involved in the acquisition of language. The stakes of this debate are very important when we consider other aspects of our evolution, such as tool manufacture and social behaviors—cases in which learning and genetics are intricately involved with the development of our brains. ■

Important Terms

plasticity: the ability of the developing brain, especially in children aged 1 to 4, to learn the sounds and grammatical structure of any human language.

spandrel: characteristic that is a byproduct of the evolution of some other character rather than a direct product of adaptive selection.

Suggested Reading

Pinker, *The Language Instinct*.

Savage-Rumbaugh and Lewin, *Kanzi*.

Questions to Consider

1. What are some other examples of human features that seem to be evolutionary "spandrels"?

2. Are there limits to the relevance of animal experiments in language learning?

Why Did Humans Start Creating Art?
Lecture 21

Art is one kind of phenomenon that archaeologists deem symbolic behavior. It's one of the clearest windows into the lives of ancient people. But artistic expression appears slowly in the archaeological record, and only within the last 40,000 years have there been large pictorial art. Today, artistic production of some kind is almost universal in humans. Many archaeologists consider it a hallmark of human behavior, showing our symbolic brains. Others suggest more utilitarian purposes for artistic production, dependent on social systems and networks.

Art is very special to humans because it's something that's done across the world; almost every culture has a figurative art tradition, but it's something that we don't fully understand. It's not like language where it exists everywhere in the world and it has an obvious function, although it's clearly a form of communication. We use it to contact others, to show others our mental images, and to express our ideas across time.

In the archaeological record, when people begin to make art, it's the first time that we can look into the past and get a picture of what their minds were doing. Art speaks to us in a way that stone tools and other kinds of artifacts don't. Some people dedicate their lives to art, but it's also a subtle part of all of our lives—there's hardly anything that we produce that doesn't involve art in some way.

Art speaks to us in a way that stone tools and other kinds of artifacts don't.

So, what is the purpose of art? This is a debate that goes back to the earliest discoveries of art. Early humans shaped tools in ways that were functional, but not every aspect of the shape was functional. Some of the very earliest examples of aesthetics in the world of tools and stone are in the Acheulean technology. A very small number of the hand axes that were discovered had something special: a fossil in the center. It is not clear whether this was deliberately artistic or had some useful purpose.

When people deliberately make something that was meant to be artistic, we often describe it as nonutilitarian in terms of function. A hand ax is a tool, so it has a utilitarian function. Even if it has a fossil shell embedded in the middle of it, it is useful. In early archaeological contexts, there are also objects that are not obviously utilitarian.

For example, at a site in Germany known as Bilzingsleben, there is a piece of bone that has a series of incisions in it that were placed in a very regular pattern. There are around a dozen of them, and they're all parallel to each other. They are not cut marks that were made for a purpose; they're nonutilitarian in that sense. But were these marks used for something—for counting, perhaps? It's completely mysterious from our perspective.

When we look at the more recent part of the archaeological record, we can find a number of artifacts that have much more deliberate intention—although they're artistic, they also have a clear utilitarian function. After 100,000 years ago in Africa, we begin to find systematically carved eggshell beads made from ostrich eggshells, which are quite thick and relatively durable. We know that people ornament themselves with beads, and ornamentation is about communicating with other people—it's about status and placement in society.

At a site called Diepkloof in South Africa, however, we find ostrich eggshells that have incised lines on them in geometric patterns, which is more difficult to explain. Ethnographically, we know that ostrich eggshells are used as containers, and they are often decorated. That stylistic part of artistic representation is something that occurs everywhere that people make containers—it's a natural part of human cultural production.

It's interesting when we find objects that aren't utilitarian but that have a clear representational quality. For example, in Namibia there's a site called Apollo 11 Cave, which has a plaque with the painting of a lion. It tells us that people are interested in depicting their environment and that modern humans aren't the only ones who make decorated objects for artistic purposes.

In Neandertal sites, we find a number of symbolic objects. We find clamshells with natural holes in them that would be potentially useful for stringing together. It is also clear that Neandertals used pigment crayons to paint presumably skin or animal hide. People do that same kind of painting today; it's a natural kind of decorative behavior. The fact that Neandertals were painting is really evocative of what their society was like.

Cave art, which occurs after the Neandertals, depicts some interesting representations of the landscape in the world that ancient people were living in. The earliest known rock art site, a cave with art inside, is Chauvet Cave in France. This cave is very famous for its large pictures of lions and rhinoceroses. People were painting aspects of their environment, and by looking at them, we can imagine what they were seeing.

The lions depicted in paintings of the Chauvet Cave, for example, don't have manes, and this is the only way we learn what these creatures were like who now are extinct. There is also a magical quality to some of these artifacts. There's a painting that looks like a human figure that's hunched over with a deer's head. From paintings like these, we know that people were imagining the world in a different way from the way it existed.

The role of art in human evolution comes down to the end of our evolutionary trajectory. It's within the last 100,000 years that we find systematic representations of any kind and within the last 30,000 years that we find these interesting, intricate paintings. This means that art is probably a phenomenon that follows along with the intensification of the human population and our greater connectivity to each other.

Being human is about sharing communication and sharing an image of the world in a way that much more ancient people apparently never did. Today, art is a fundamental aspect of all of humanity, and it emerges quite recently in the archaeological record. Art tells us that, as we became human, we transformed ourselves into communicating and representing beings.

The purpose of artistic production in the past is in a sense mysterious— we will never really know why some particular objects were made. The symbolic capacities to produce art really may be central to our emergence as a worldwide species and our ability to adapt with culture to such a wide range of environments. ■

Suggested Reading

Clottes, *Cave Art*.

Guthrie, *The Nature of Paleolithic Art*.

Questions to Consider

1. Ancient sites with rock art often have ritual importance. What is the relation of art and ritual or religion?

2. How do humans use art or ornamental objects today to mark themselves or send messages to other people about their social importance?

Clovis or Pre-Clovis?
Lecture 22

In the 19th century, many anthropologists thought that humans had a long antiquity in the Americas. Ales Hrdlicka argued that humans had not existed here in the deep past but had migrated from Asia after the Ice Ages. Ancient artifacts from the Midwest, known as Clovis points, mark an early culture that was thought to be the first in the Americas. But a handful of archaeological sites during the last 20 years have shown that people reached the Americas as early as 2000 years before Clovis.

When and how the earliest people arrived in North America and dispersed into South America is a debate that concerns timing. This arrival occurred either before or with the appearance of an archaeological culture called the **Clovis** culture, which existed about 14,000 years ago. If humans arrived in North America at that time, the Clovis culture could represent the earliest Americans. Some archaeologists disagree, claiming that people reached the New World earlier and that there are some sites that show a pre-Clovis occupation.

This debate goes back to the beginnings of physical anthropology as a discipline. Physical anthropologist Ales Hrdlicka had decided by 1903 that there was nothing in the New World that had the kind of great antiquity that the archaeological record in the Old World was producing. By examining the archaeological record in the New World, he found skeletal resemblances between New World and Asian people and deduced that early Americans had dispersed from Asia across an ancient land bridge into the Americas.

Because the archaeological record seemed to be relatively recent in the New World, Hrdlicka believed that this event had happened recently, probably since the last glaciation. He used the Bering land bridge theory—that people had come from Asia and entered the New World at the end of the last Ice Age—to guide his studies. He searched for so-called ancient skeletal remains in the New World and tested his scenario for a recent migration. If people had been in the New World longer ago than the last Ice Age, then they would've left remains that were deeper and had greater antiquity.

Hrdlicka went to site after site in the New World and demonstrated that each specimen couldn't have the great antiquity that had been claimed. He examined a skeleton that became known as the Lansing Man from Lansing, Kansas, and determined that it was probably more recent than had been thought because the specimen did not seem to be fossilized at all. Through all Hrdlicka's examinations, there was never any demonstration that anything was here earlier than could've been the case if people had arrived recently over the Bering land bridge.

In order to get to the New World, people had to be able to occupy the northernmost tier of Asia. Then, they must've traveled to Siberia, working with the climate that existed in Siberia and in the exposed Bering land strait in Alaska, the region that has become known as Beringia. It turns out we know something about how long ago people were able to occupy the environment in Beringia because of archaeological sites in the northernmost parts of Siberia that date to before 30,000 years ago.

The first New World people that we have archaeological evidence of are big game hunters who used a kind of distance projectile weapon technology, Clovis-type technology. Clovis is named after a place in New Mexico, which is one of the first places where they found this type of artifact, which is now called an **atlatl**, or spear thrower. An atlatl has a long handle that has either a hole or a little cup in it, in which sits a dart with a point at one end.

The Clovis artifact that's most recognizable is a very long spear. The **Clovis point**, as it's called today, is very recognizable and is found across the western Midwest of the United States. We know a lot about the way that people made these Clovis points because we can trace and chemically analyze the raw material they used to make them to figure out where they must've come from.

Clovis points have been found sometimes hundreds of miles away from the source of the raw material, which tells us that these people were highly mobile. We don't find very dense accumulations of their tools except in the extreme southeastern United States and in Texas, which tells us that they might have settled in this area first before following herds.

Some people believe that the Clovis population's effect on these herds of large animals was so great that they drove them to extinction, which is the basis of the **overkill hypothesis**—the idea that humans have such an impact on large animals, such as mammoths and mastodons, that they become extinct.

Archaeologists and paleontologists still debate this idea: Were humans primarily responsible, or was climate change the key factor? It's probably that both of these factors were working together. Regardless, it's clear that the Clovis technology represents a technology that supports the idea of traveling from Siberia to Beringia because it is highly effective in its ability to expand across large areas.

We just don't have the skeletal evidence that represents what are potentially the earliest people in the New World.

The problem with this scenario is that we don't have very much clear skeletal evidence of the earliest people in the New World. In fact, the skeletons that we have tend to date rather later. The Clovis technology dates to between about 13,200 years ago and about 12,800 years ago at its maximum extent—about a 500-year span sometime after 14,000 years ago. Skeletal evidence is very rare in the New World until after 12,000 years ago.

We just don't have the skeletal evidence that represents what are potentially the earliest people in the New World. The skeletons that we do have are similar to today's Native American people in some respects. These skeletons are also similar to those of Asians that lived in northern China at around the same time, which indicates that the population changed from the earliest inhabitants of the New World up to today's American Indians.

In addition to this, there are some sites where we find tools in well-stratified layers that appear to be older than Clovis. One of the most celebrated of these is Meadowcroft Rockshelter, which is in Pennsylvania. This site has tools that are in a layer that's about 15,000 years old, which is older than Clovis. These tools are simpler than Clovis artifacts, so we know they did not come from this population. The dating of this site, however, is debated.

The evidence for some pre-Clovis habitation of North America, and possibly South America, is now well accepted. But this was not a very long time before the Clovis culture, only 2000 years or so. The movement of people from Siberia into Alaska is still not well understood. It is possible that the earliest people skirted the coasts, using boats, and settled the interior of Alaska and Canada relatively later. ■

Important Terms

atlatl: weapon that uses leverage to achieve greater velocity in dart throwing.

Clovis: prehistoric Paleo-Indian culture that first appears 13,000 years ago in North America at the end of the last glacial period that is characterized by the manufacture of "Clovis points" and distinctive bone and ivory tools.

Clovis point: thin, fluted projectile point created using bifacial percussion flaking associated with the North American Clovis culture.

overkill hypothesis: hypothesis that humans were responsible for the Late Pleistocene extinction of megafauna, such as woolly mammoths and mastodons, in northern Eurasia and North and South America.

Suggested Reading

Haynes, *The Early Settlement of North America*.

Relethford, *Reflections of Our Past*.

Questions to Consider

1. The migration of people into the Americas was only one of many ancient colonizations—other examples include Australia and the Pacific islands. Are there common features to these large-scale movements?

2. The debate between Clovis-first and pre-Clovis advocates has intensified, even as evidence for a few pre-Clovis sites has become stronger in recent years. Why does this debate matter?

Farming—Migration or Diffusion?
Lecture 23

We know that agriculture originated in a few places—including Mesopotamia and China in the Old World, Mexico and Peru in the New World—and spread to other areas. But how did this spread happen? Did the early agriculturalists grow their populations and migrate outward, carrying farming with them? Or did neighboring hunter-gatherers adopt farming practices by learning them from the farmers, thereby growing their own populations? This debate goes back to the 19th century. Today, genetic and linguistic evidence add to this debate.

The origin of farming is a relatively recent event in human evolution, initiating around 10,000 years ago at the very end of the last Ice Age. Farming is a fundamental shift in the human subsistence pattern that imposes many other kinds of changes on human societies and, as a result, on human biology. Humans begin to live more sedentary, defending their farmed territory, and they begin to store foods for longer periods of time because of alternating growing seasons and winters.

Did ancient people migrate from the centers of agriculture into other places, or did they learn how to grow crops from their neighbors and adopt the process themselves? The idea that agriculture originated in one place and spread from there is referred to as the **cultural diffusion model**. This debate over migration versus diffusion is, again, one of the oldest in anthropology.

In Germany, a farming culture existed around 5000 years ago called the **Linearbandkeramik** culture, which is often abbreviated LBK. It's one of the earliest agricultural cultures in Europe, and we now know it was a dairying culture as well. Because we know that agriculture isn't original to Europe, we know that this culture was using ideas that came from West Asia. In the 19th century, physical anthropologists studied the skulls of these people to determine whether they were biologically related to earlier Europeans or whether they had come from somewhere else.

These Neolithic people are different from living people in many ways. Anthropologists examined the features of these skeletons, but they also considered how those features changed over time; in fact, their brains got smaller. The morphology of the skull also changed; it became thinner over time. Even more radically, the skull changed in its proportion of length to width—longer and narrower compared to ours.

Even though these Neolithic people did seem to shrink in body size due to nutritional availability, their brains were shrinking more than predicted from body size. In other words, the population was changing biologically at the same time that it is unclear whether people were migrating. This issue of brain shrinking is an argument in favor of the idea that there was a biological shift that's related to people migrating from somewhere else.

The first explanation for this biological change was migration. The idea was that there had originally been broadheaded and longheaded races of people that lived in different places. The long heads moved in to Europe from somewhere else, and later, the broad heads expanded their population from the south into the north. This was an explanation of the variability within Europe today and also of the shift over time in the movement of people.

This was the root of the idea of migration in anthropology—the idea that when farming shows up in Europe, it's because people were bringing it from somewhere else, and those people have different proportions, which is reflected in the skeletal record.

The case for this idea would be even stronger if this trend toward broader heads were unique to Europe. However, this phenomenon occurs basically everywhere that people lived. It's not exactly the same everywhere, and it does seem to exist more in agricultural places. This raises the possibility that this is not a shift due to the migration of people, but it's a shift due to the evolution of people. If this skeletal change is reflecting evolution, then there's no need to posit the idea that people are migrating from somewhere else—you could have them changing where they lived.

Geneticists began to consider how we could relate the pattern of genetic changes to the skeletal changes and how we could compare genetic changes to other kinds of changes. The most prominent kind of change that people were really interested in explaining was language change. A current hypothesis connects the spread of ancient languages with farming, which stands out as something that would be strong enough to bring people, grow their population, cause them to move, and establish themselves in new places.

Luca Cavalli-Sforza, a famous Italian geneticist, hypothesized that the spread of people was responsible for the spread of agriculture. In other words, people's genes were dispersing through Europe, and they were bringing with them agricultural technology, but they were also mixing with the people who were already there—an idea he called the **demic diffusion model**. Basically, it's a mixture of migration and diffusion. Other parts of the world also saw population movements and the founding of new populations after agriculture was invented.

In Europe, the situation has become more clouded recently due to the sampling of ancient skeletons' DNA. Genetically, there's a prediction: If there's a diffusion of agriculture into Europe, then the ancient people who lived before farming ought to be genetically like the people who lived there when farming was introduced, and presumably, those people should look like us.

> It seems that populations have the ability to grow and shift and replace each other much more quickly than we might've imagined.

In fact, the sampling of the genes of these ancient people shows that they're different from the people who were there before them, and the LBK people are different from the people who lived there after them. In other words, it's not one movement of people; it seems to be 2 movements of people.

It seems that populations have the ability to grow and shift and replace each other much more quickly than we might've imagined. It's not just one factor like the introduction of farming that can influence this; it's multiple factors, including possibly the language shift, warfare, or the introduction of new crops and animals.

Many other regions of the world have seen the spread of agriculturalists from their initial sources. In some areas, migration is also a much more important mechanism for population growth and the spread of technology than is exchange. It seems that the package of farming technology comes together and is hard to learn and transmit. The reasons for population growth are connected to the importance of adaptation in genes. ■

Important Terms

cultural diffusion model: spread of language and culture (e.g., agriculture) by cultural impact between populations involving limited genetic exchange between them.

demic diffusion model: spread of language and culture (e.g., agriculture) by gradual movement of populations and interbreeding with earlier inhabitants.

Linearbandkeramik (a.k.a. **LBK**): the Neolithic Linear Pottery culture that flourished between 5500 and 4500 years ago in central Europe. Its pottery is characterized by decorative patterns of painted and incised lines.

Suggested Reading

Cochran and Harpending, *The 10,000 Year Explosion*.

Relethford, *Reflections of Our Past*.

Questions to Consider

1. Can the appearance and spread of farming serve as an analogy for earlier population events among hunter-gatherers? Or do the larger, more sedentary populations of farmers make them a poor model for foragers?

2. Many anthropologists were surprised when ancient DNA showed that the Neolithic population of Europe was quite different from earlier and later people. Are there other events in history that might show a similar pattern of change?

Are Humans Still Evolving?
Lecture 24

Many scientists over the years have suggested that human evolution has stopped, or will stop soon, as we change our environment to make life easier and as medical technology allows people to survive who would otherwise have died. Recent genetic evidence suggests that during the past 10,000 years our evolution actually accelerated—but what about today? Is our evolution really stopping, or is it continuing? Is it changing direction?

What is the role of natural selection in our population in the recent past and today? Is evolution slowing down in humans, or is evolution continuing or even speeding up in our species? We've known for a long time that during the course of the last few thousand years there have been biological changes in humans. We see changes in the skeleton—the kinds of changes in the shape and size of the skull—when we look at skeletal samples of people from before the development of agriculture, from around the time of agriculture, and in more recent samples of people of agriculturalists.

Is evolution slowing down in humans, or is evolution continuing or even speeding up in our species?

What has become clear in the last few years is that these changes in skeletal form are accompanied by other massive changes in genetics. A very good example of this is a gene called lactase, which is an enzyme that allows you to digest a sugar called lactose. That sugar only naturally occurs in milk, so it's a sugar that if you're not a milk drinker you don't have access to. Every human is a milk drinker sometime in his or her life, just as all mammals are, because milk is the natural nutrition that babies get when they're born.

Most mammals turn this enzyme off after they are weaned, but some humans leave it on and continue to make that enzyme as they're adults, which causes a condition called **lactase persistence**. These humans are mutants because they actually have new mutations that keep this enzyme active. That mutation occurs only in human populations that have a long history of keeping and domesticating dairy animals.

The environment these humans have created, where milk is available to them as adults, has selected for their ability to continue to digest the milk as adults. This genetic change is one of the most rapid genetic changes that has happened in the human population, and it's common today in parts of the world with a history of dairying.

There are many human phenotypes that we can point at that are subject to this recent pattern of selection, especially those that are associated with pigmentation. In Europe today, people are light skinned whereas in Africa they're dark skinned. Dark skinned is the ancestral form for humans. The light-skinned version that is in Europe is something that has emerged within the past 20,000 years. We know that because of the many genetic variants that affect pigmentation that are new and that occur in Europe today.

There are many different gene variants that have emerged over a very short period of time, and when we consider pigmentation as a system which involves more than a dozen genes that have changed in Europe and a similar number that have changed in China, those genes are all relatively new. It's a sign of the rapid change in our population.

The most potent explanation for this kind of rapid genetic change is the growth of the human population. The more people that exist, the more mutations there are to choose from. As the population grows, there is more and more of a chance of something beneficial happening. If we look across the human genome, the reason why today we have a lot of genetic changes that have unfolded in the recent past is because there are so many people in the recent past.

The climate and environments that we've created for ourselves have encouraged those kinds of genetic changes. For example, malaria is a disease that has greatly intensified in the past few thousand years—not only because the parasite has adapted, but also because people have made a habitat for mosquitoes by farming, which has enabled the spread of malaria.

When we think about how human evolution has gone in the past few thousand years, we have to see that even though cultures have massively adapted us to the environment in new ways, creating new opportunities for us, they have also created new selection on us. They've given us the environment that has prompted us to evolve even more rapidly.

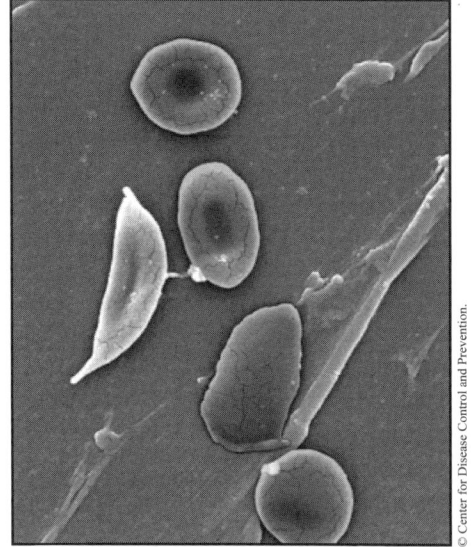

Over a million years ago, humans evolved to become immune to the kind of malaria that commonly affects chimpanzees today.

Today, we live in a population where we have medical treatment that's reducing the importance of many diseases on us. We live in a population where people are living on average into their 70s and 80s. This is long past the age when they could reproduce, so there's not a lot of mortality that's selecting on people today. Is it possible that our culture has really stopped our evolution from happening?

Natural selection is still happening in our population, but it's happening not because people are dying young, but because people are having more or less kids, depending on what kinds of traits they have. If people have kids younger and have more of them, then if there are any genes that are associated with having kids younger, those genes will be predominant in the population in the next generation. There's an accumulation over time, and that's the effect of natural selection.

Given that we're currently evolving in some respects at least, a natural question is: Where are we going in the future? It's always hazardous to predict where things are going in evolution because where they're going depends on the environment, which constantly changes. In other words, we need to know something about the environment in the future to make predictions about what's going to happen in the future.

However, we can make a few predictions. Because migration between places rapidly increased and people are mixing their population more than in the past, in the future our population should be less diverse in terms of different places, but more diverse within each place because we're bringing together genes from many parts of the world.

Today, genetic testing companies are rapidly developing ways to assess the gene variants that people carry, and one of the main reasons for this is because they want to develop tests that will assess the risks that people have in conceiving children. Because that technology is increasing, we can predict that evolution will come more and more under our control. Whether genes persist in the population will be conditioned on whether people choose to have offspring with those genes.

The course of our evolution over the last 6 million years has brought us from something that is basically apelike up to today's variation of humans. That course of evolution has followed many channels, and each channel has its own story, but all of those stories were guided by the processes in the environment. Today, our story is very much more guided by the processes of human society and choice, and we really have made a transition into a different pattern of change. Nature still imposes itself on us, but natural selection will become synonymous with cultural selection as we start to become more technological in the sense of genetics and evolution. ■

Important Term

lactase persistence: the ability of adults to drink milk due to a gene mutation that permanently switches on the lactase gene that exists in European dairy regions and that probably originated only about 5000 years ago.

Suggested Reading

Cochran and Harpending, *The 10,000 Year Explosion*.

Questions to Consider

1. Why is it so hard for scientists to predict the direction of evolutionary change in the future?

2. The rapid evolution of genes in the last 10,000 years was in part driven by differences in mortality and in part by differences in fertility. Considering these evolutionary changes, which ones seem to reduce mortality? Which may have increased fertility?

Timeline

14 million years ago (mya) .... *Kenyapithecus wickeri* (Fort Ternan, Kenya.)

8–12 mya .... *Sivapithecus*.

c. 10 mya .... *Ramapithecus*.

8–10 mya .... *Oreopithecus bambolii* (Tuscany, Italy).

7 mya .... *Sahelanthropus tchadensis* (Toros-Menalla, Chad).

6 mya .... *Orrorin tugenensis* (Lukeino, Kenya).

5.5 mya .... *Ardipithecus kadabba*.

4.5–4.3 mya .... *Ardipithecus ramidus*.

4.4 mya .... Ardi (ARA-VP 6/500), Aramis, Ethiopia.

4.2–3.9 mya .... *Australopithecus anamensis*.

3.9 mya .... Woranso-Mille, Ethiopia.

c. 3.9–2.9 mya .... *Australopithecus afarensis*.

3.5–3.7 mya .... Laetoli, Tanzania.

c. 3.4 mya .... Dikika, Ethiopia; Dikika, Ethiopia (possible cutmarks); Dikika, Ethiopia (*Australopithecus afarensis* hyoid).

Timeline

3.4–3.0 mya	Hadar, Ethiopia.
3.2 mya	Lucy (AL 288-1), Hadar, Ethiopia.
2.8 mya	Taung, South Africa.
2.8 mya	Earliest robust australopithecines (Omo, Ethiopia).
2.8–2.0 mya	*Australopithecus africanus*.
2.6 mya	Earliest stone tools (Gona, Ethiopia).
2.5 mya	Bouri, Ethiopia (tools).
2.5 mya	Black Skull (KNM-WT 17000), West Turkana, Kenya.
2.5–2.0 mya	Omo, Ethiopia (possible *Homo* teeth and jaws).
c. 2.5–1.5 mya	*Australopithecus boisei*.
2.4 mya	Hadar, Ethiopia (tools); Hadar, Ethiopia (AL 666 *Homo* maxilla).
2.2 mya	Kanjera, Kenya.
2.2 mya	Sterkfontein, South Africa (member 4).
2 mya	Malapa, South Africa.
c. 2.0–1.5 mya	*Homo habilis*.
c. 2.0–1.4 mya (?)	*Australopithecus robustus*.
1.9 mya	KNM-ER 1470 (Koobi Fora, Kenya).

1.9–1.5 mya .... Koobi Fora, Kenya (*Homo habilis* fossils).

1.9–1.2 mya (or less) .... Swartkrans, South Africa.

1.8 mya .... Dmanisi, Republic of Georgia.

1.8 mya .... Mojokerto, Java.

1.8 mya .... First *Homo erectus* in Java (Mojokerto).

1.5–1.8 mya .... Olduvai Gorge (*Homo habilis* fossils).

800,000–1.8 mya .... Olduvai Gorge, Tanzania.

c. 1.8 mya–
400,000 years ago (ya) .... *Homo erectus*.

1.65 mya .... KNM-ER 3833 (Ileret, Kenya).

1.6 mya .... Olduvai Gorge, Tanzania (OH 5).

1.5 mya .... Nariokotome, Kenya.

1.5 mya–300,000 ya .... Acheulean industry.

1.0–1.2 mya .... Trinil, Java (Indonesia).

1.0 mya .... Gongwangling, China.

1 mya .... First archaeology in Soa Basin, Flores.

500,000–800,000 ya .... Zhoukoudian, China.

600,000 ya .... Boxgrove, England.

600,000 ya .... Last Yellowstone eruption.

500,000–600,000 ya	Sima de los Huesos, Atapuerca, Spain.
500,000 ya	Mauer, Germany.
300,000–400,000 ya	Swanscombe, England.
c. 250,000–400,000 ya	Neandertal-Denisova-human common ancestor.
250,000–300,000 ya	Petralona, Greece.
250,000 ya	Steinheim, Germany.
c. 200,000–250,000 ya	Ehringsdorf, Germany.
200,000 ya (?)	Kanam, Kenya.
c. 200,000 ya	mtDNA "Eve," human mtDNA common ancestor.
c. 200,000–30,000 ya	Mousterian industry.
200,000–30,000 ya	Neandertals.
190,000 ya	Omo Kibish, Ethiopia.
165,000 ya	Herto, Ethiopia.
120,000 ya	Tabun, Israel.
120,000 ya	Krapina, Croatia.
100,000 ya	Skhul, Israel.
90,000–100,000 ya	Qafzeh, Israel.

94,000 ya	Earliest archaeological level of Liang Bua Cave.
74,000 ya	Toba megaeruption.
70,000 ya	Blombos incised rock.
60,000 ya	Oldest ostrich eggshell art (Diepkloof Cave, South Africa).
60,000 ya	Kebara, Israel.
c. 50,000–60,000 ya	La Chapelle-Aux-Saints, France.
50,000–60,000 ya	El Sidron, Spain.
c. 50,000 ya	Denisova Cave genome.
c. 40,000–50,000 ya	Human habitation of Australia.
c. 45,000 ya	Shanidar, Iraq.
45,000–30,000 ya	Vindija Cave (Croatia).
c. 45,000–25,000 ya	Aurignacian.
c. 45,000–10,000 ya	Upper Paleolithic.
c. 40,000 ya	Oldest Australian rock art.
30,000–35,000 ya	Mezmaiskaya, Russia.
30,000 ya	Apollo 11 lion plaque, Namibia.
30,000 ya	Chauvet Cave, France.
24,000 ya	Lascaux, France.

Timeline

18,000 ya	LB 1 skeleton.
c. 15,000 ya	Bernifal, France.
14,400 ya	Paisley Cave coprolite, Oregon.
14,000 ya	Earliest Monte Verde industry, Chile.
12,000–13,000 ya	Clovis industry.
c. 10,000 ya	Earliest evidence of farming in Near East.
c. 9000 ya	Kennewick skeleton.
c. 8000 ya	Origin of lactase persistence allele.
c. 6000–7500 ya	LBK (Linearbandkeramik) culture.
c. 5000–6000 ya	Dispersal of Lapita pottery culture into western Polynesia.
c. 3500–4500 ya	Early Bronze Age.

Glossary

Acheulean technology: Archaeological industry of stone tool manufacture associated with *Homo habilis* from about 1.8 million years ago that is characterized by oval- and pear-shaped hand axes.

allele: One of 2 or more forms of a gene. Different alleles can result in different traits, such as color.

allometry: The study of the relationship of body size to shape, anatomy, physiology, and behavior.

alpha-tectorin: Protein found in the inner ear, as part of a structure called the tectorial membrane, which helps to convert sound waves to nerve impulses—a critical process for hearing.

Ardipithecus: Hominin that is 4.4 to 5.5 million years old. Arguably the oldest known hominin yet to be discovered, it is bipedal, has a small brain, and has a grasping big toe for climbing.

assisted reproductive technology: Method used to achieve pregnancy by artificial or partially artificial means.

atlatl: Weapon that uses leverage to achieve greater velocity in dart throwing.

Aurignacian technology: Toolmaking industry and artistic tradition of Upper Paleolithic Europe whose main feature is its heavy use of core and blade technology, including a more efficient flake removal system.

Australopithecus: Genus of ape on the ancestral line leading to humanity.

Australopithecus afarensis: Hominin that existed 3.9 to 2.9 million years ago ("Lucy") and was discovered by Tim White and Don Johanson at Hadar,

Ethiopia, in 1978. Originally thought to be ancestral to modern humans, this hominin is gracile, bipedal, and has a small brain.

Australopithecus africanus: Early hominid discovered by Raymond Dart near Taung in South Africa in 1924. Itlived 2 to 3 million years ago in the Pliocene. Like the older *Australopithecus afarensis*, *Australopithecus africanus* is often classed as a gracile australopithecine because it lacks the very large jaws and teeth of the robust australopithecines.

Australopithecus robustus: Fossil hominin that is 2.3 to 1.3 million years old and was discovered by Robert Broom in South Africa in 1938. Its jaw musculature, mandible, and teeth are larger than *Australopithecus afarensis* or *Australopithecus africanus*.

Australopithecus sediba: Species of *Australopithecus* that existed between 1.95 and 1.78 million years ago in the early Pleistocene and was discovered by Lee Berger in South Africa.

bifacial tool: Stone tool sharpened on 2 sides and used as a multipurpose knife or hand ax.

bipedality: Walking on 2 legs.

Broca's area: Region of the hominid brain with functions linked to speech production.

caldera: Cauldron-like volcanic feature that is usually formed by the collapse of land following a volcanic eruption.

chert: Hard, crystalline rock that was often used in prehistoric times as a raw material for the construction of stone tools.

chopper: A rock from which several large flakes have been broken in order to produce a sharp edge or point. It is a characteristic tool of Oldowan technology.

chopping tool technology: Stone tool-making industry producing sharp flakes and shaped core chopping tools that was prevalent in the Oldowan, but particularly in what are now China and Southeast Asia. This technology existed for about 1.5 million years without a significant change.

cladistics: Method of classifying species of organisms into groups that consist of an ancestor organism and all of its descendants (and nothing else). The intent is to reflect the relative recency of common ancestry or the sharing of similar features.

cladogram: Diagram used in cladistics that shows ancestral relations between organisms to represent the evolutionary tree of life.

Clovis: Prehistoric Paleo-Indian culture that first appears 13,000 years ago in North America at the end of the last glacial period that is characterized by the manufacture of "Clovis points" and distinctive bone and ivory tools.

Clovis point: Thin, fluted projectile point created using bifacial percussion flaking associated with the North American Clovis culture.

cochlea: Spiral-shaped auditory portion of the inner ear.

cultural diffusion model: Spread of language and culture (e.g., agriculture) by cultural impact between populations involving limited genetic exchange between them.

demic diffusion model: Spread of language and culture (e.g., agriculture) by gradual movement of populations and interbreeding with earlier inhabitants.

dental attrition: Wearing down of the teeth caused by grinding abrasive foods such as seeds, nuts, and grasses.

dietary hypothesis: The hypothesis that gracile australopithecines had access to higher-quality food sources such as fruit and meat, while robust australopithecines were confined to lower-quality foods such as roots and grasses.

embryo selection: Process of taking eggs from a female and fertilizing them in vitro.

endocast: Internal mold of the cranial vault, used in paleoanthropology to study brain size and structure.

ephemeral scatter: Location where stone tools and fragments reveal a gathering of prehistoric hominins for the purpose of a cooperative activity such as toolmaking or animal butchery.

extractive foraging: Locating and/or processing embedded foods, such as underground roots and insects or hard-shelled nuts and fruits, with probes or other tools.

fallback food hypothesis: The hypothesis that in times of plenty, gracile and robust australopithecines both had access to high-quality food sources such as fruit and meat, but in scarcity, robust australopithecines used lower-quality foods such as roots and grasses as a "fallback" diet, while gracile types looked harder for fruit and meat.

flaked core: Stone from which flakes have been knocked off to produce a sharp edge to use as a tool.

FoxP2 gene: A gene involved in early brain development. The normal form of this gene in humans appears to be important for language development.

genetic engineering: Direct manipulation of an organism's genetic material in a way that does not occur under natural conditions that involves the use of recombinant DNA techniques.

genetic variation: Differences in genes brought about by mutation, providing the "raw material" for natural selection.

genome sequencing: Laboratory process that determines the complete DNA sequence of an organism's genome—the order of As, Cs, Gs, and Ts that make up an organism's DNA. The human genome is made up of over 3 billion of these genetic letters.

geographic determinism: Theory that the human habits and characteristics of a particular culture are shaped by geographic conditions.

gracile: Hominins having a smaller skull, a slender bone structure, and teeth suited for tearing meat.

hammer stone: Hand-held stone tool used as a prehistoric hammer to strike or fracture another object.

hobbit: Nickname for *Homo floresiensis*, a dwarf-like hominin living on the Island of Flores until about 13,000 years ago.

hominin (a.k.a. **hominid**): A member of the human lineage, more closely related to living people than to chimpanzees or other living primates. This group was formerly called the "hominids," but "hominid" now technically refers to humans, chimpanzees, gorillas, and their relatives. Living and fossil apes, including chimpanzees, gorillas, gibbons, orangutans, and humans are called hominoids.

Homo: Genus that includes modern humans and extinct species such as *Homo habilis* and *Homo erectus*, which are closely related to humans. This genus is descended from *Australopithecus* and is estimated to be about 2.3 to 2.4 million years old.

Homo erectus: Species of hominin that originated in Africa—and spread as far as China and Java—from the end of the Pliocene Epoch to the later Pleistocene, about 1.8 to 1.3 million years ago.

Homo ergaster: A name for African fossil humans that existed between around 1.8 to 1.5 million years ago and that may be an ancestral population for all later humans. Most paleoanthropologists would call these fossils African *Homo erectus*.

Homo floresiensis: Dwarf-like hominins living on the Island of Flores until about 13,000 years ago.

Homo habilis: Hominin that existed 2.3 to 1.4 million years ago and was discovered by Mary and Louis Leakey in Tanzania that used primitive stone tools (thus "handy man").

Homo heidelbergensis: Hominin that existed between 600,000 and 400,000 years ago and that may be a direct ancestor of both *Homo neanderthalensis* in Europe and *Homo sapiens*. These hominins used a stone tool technology similar to Acheulean. Many paleoanthropologists see this as a synonym for "archaic *Homo sapiens*."

Homo rudolfensis: Hominin that existed 1.9 million years ago and was discovered by Richard and Maeve Leakey at Lake Turkana, Kenya. Many paleoanthropologists would view this as a synonym for *Homo habilis*.

human genome project: A 13-year project, completed in 2003, to identify all of the 20,000 to 25,000 genes in human DNA and to determine the sequences of the 3 billion chemical base pairs that make up human DNA.

hyoid bone: Horseshoe-shaped bone situated in the neck that serves as an anchoring structure for the larynx. It is critical for speech production.

insular dwarfism: Reduction in size of large animals—including humans—when their population's gene pool is limited to a very small environment, occurring primarily on islands.

Java Man: *Homo erectus* hominin that is 1 million years old and was discovered at Trinil, east Java, Indonesia, by Eugène Dubois.

Kenyanthropus: Hominin fossil that existed 3.5 to 3.2 million years ago and was discovered in Lake Turkana, Kenya, in 1999 by Maeve Leakey's team.

Kenyapithecus: Fossil ape that is 14 million years old and was discovered by Louis Leakey in 1961 at a site called Fort Ternan in Kenya.

lactase persistence: The ability of adults to drink milk due to a gene mutation that permanently switches on the lactase gene that exists in European dairy regions and that probably originated only about 5000 years ago.

Linearbandkeramik (a.k.a. **LBK**): The Neolithic Linear Pottery culture that flourished between 5500 and 4500 years ago in central Europe. Its pottery is characterized by decorative patterns of painted and incised lines.

living floor: Level of an archaeological site where humans lived, as indicated by a scatter of stone tools, animal bones, and other artifacts.

lunate sulcus: A crescent-shaped groove on the occipital part of the brain. In fossil endocasts, when it can be determined, it may serve as a potential marker of cognitive evolution.

manuport: A naturally occurring object that's been deliberately moved for some reason to a new location. It is evidence that hominins were selecting objects or materials for specific purposes rather than just using what comes to hand.

mastoid process: The bony process behind the ear to which several muscles attach. It is typically smaller in Neandertals than in modern humans.

microcephaly: Abnormally small size of the skull and brain.

Miocene: Geological epoch that extends from about 23 to 5.3 million years ago. It was a time of warmer global climates, when as many as 100 species of apes roamed throughout the Old World.

mitochondrial DNA: The DNA found in organelles called mitochondria that is located outside of the cell nucleus and is inherited only from the mother. Mitochondrial DNA is a powerful tool for tracking ancestry through females and has been used in this role to track human ancestry back hundreds of generations. It includes only around 16,000 base pairs as opposed to the 3 billion in a copy of the nuclear genome.

molecular clock: Technique in molecular evolution that infers the time that species diverged from each other based on the amount of genetic difference and the rate of molecular change over time.

morphology: Study of the form and structure of organisms and their specific structural features.

Movius line: Theoretical boundary line across Eurasia separating Paleolithic hand ax industries in the west from those without hand axes in the east that was proposed in 1948 by Hallam Movius.

multiregional hypothesis: The hypothesis that modern humans evolved from a population of archaic humans (including Neandertals and *Homo erectus*) that was spread across much of the Old World by a process of selection and genetic exchange.

Neandertal: Fossil hominin that existed 150,000 to 30,000 years ago and were our closest extinct relatives. These hominins had large brains, used tools, and hunted and probably coexisted with *Homo sapiens*.

Neandertal bonus: The fact that about 1 to 4% of the DNA of non-Africans today comes from Neandertals.

neutral theory of molecular evolution: Theory that the vast majority of evolutionary changes at the molecular level are caused by a random drift of mutations that are not under selection.

occipital bun: Prominent bulge, or projection, of the occipital bone at the back of the skull that is characteristic of Neandertals and some modern humans.

Oldowan technology: Earliest stone tool industry in prehistory, being used from 2.6 million years ago up until 1.7 million years ago. Stones were shaped to be choppers, scrapers, and pounders and were used by *Homo habilis* and *Homo ergaster*.

Oreopithecus: An ancient genus of extinct apes that lived around 10 to 8 million years ago on an ancient island that included parts of present-day Tuscany and Sardinia.

out of Africa hypothesis: Hypothesis that all modern humans stem from a single group of *Homo sapiens* who emigrated from Africa within the last

100,000 years, mostly replacing other early humans (such as Neandertals) rather than interbreeding with them.

overkill hypothesis: Hypothesis that humans were responsible for the Late Pleistocene extinction of megafauna, such as woolly mammoths and mastodons, in northern Eurasia and North and South America.

paleoanthropology: Study of ancient humans.

paleosol: An ancient soil structure preserved by burial, often underneath river flood sediments or volcanic ash.

parallelism: The evolution of geographically separated groups in such a way that they show morphological resemblances.

Peking Man: Hominin that existed 770,000 to 230,000 years ago (*Homo erectus*) that was found at Zhoukoudian, near Beijing, by Davidson Black.

petrous portion: A pyramid-shaped part of the temporal bone that encloses the middle and inner ear. It is one of the hardest parts of the skeleton.

phyletic dwarfism: Dwarfism caused by evolution.

Piltdown Man: A "discovery" in 1912 in England that was believed to be the "missing link" between apes and humans by the majority of the scientific community. In 1953, it was proven to be a hoax.

Pithecanthropus erectus: Original name for Java Man, who is now considered to be *Homo erectus*.

plasticity: The ability of the developing brain, especially in children aged 1 to 4, to learn the sounds and grammatical structure of any human language.

Pleistocene: Geological epoch that extends from about 2.6 million to about 12,000 years ago. At the height of the Pleistocene glacial ages, more than 30% of the land area of the Earth was covered by glacial ice; during the interglacial stages, probably only about 10% was covered. The animals of the Pleistocene began to resemble those of today, and new groups of land mammals, including humans, appeared. At the end of the epoch, mass extinctions occurred.

Pliocene: Geological epoch that extends from about 5.3 to 2.6 million years ago. It was a time of global cooling after the warmer Miocene, and the first recognizable hominins, the australopithecines, appeared during this time.

polycentric hypothesis: The name for Franz Weidenreich's hypothesis that modern humans came into existence by the interaction of several ancient centers of evolution—chiefly Africa, Asia, and Europe.

polygenism: Theory of human origins positing that the human races had distinct origins.

population bottleneck: An evolutionary event in which a population is limited to a very small number of individuals for a significant time. A bottleneck can cause inbreeding in a population and may be an explanation for why human mitochondrial variation is very limited.

preneandertal hypothesis: Hypothesis that a preneandertal hominin was the direct ancestor of both Neandertals and *Homo sapiens*, diverging about 200,000 years ago.

presapiens hypothesis: Hypothesis that Neandertals and *Homo sapiens* had separate lineages long before 200,000 years ago.

Proconsul: Extinct genus of primates that existed from 23 to 15 million years ago during the early Miocene Epoch.

Ramapithecus: Fossil primate genus that lived around 10 to 8 million years ago and was once thought to be the first direct ancestor of modern humans but now recognized as a synonym of *Sivapithecus*.

robust: Hominins having a larger skull, a larger bone structure, and teeth suited for grinding seeds and nuts.

Sahelanthropus: Extinct hominin species from about 7 million years ago.

sexual dimorphism: Difference in form between individuals of different sex in the same species that may lead to confusion when few fossil specimens are available.

shovel shaped: The distinctive shape of upper incisor teeth, in which the edges of the teeth have ridges that give them the overall shape of a coal shovel. Shovel-shaped incisors are common in East Asia today and are shared with some fossil humans in that region.

Sivapithecus: Fossil primate genus dating from the Miocene Epoch (23.7 to 5.3 million years ago) and thought to be the direct ancestor of the orangutan.

spandrel: Characteristic that is a byproduct of the evolution of some other character rather than a direct product of adaptive selection.

stemmed-point technology: Stone tool technology that added a stem to the end of a projectile weapon opposite the point for hafting onto the shaft of an arrow or spear.

stratigraphy: Study of the archaeological layers that make up an archaeological deposit to better understand the chronology and relationship of its artifacts.

taphonomy: Study of decaying organisms over time and how they become fossilized (if they do).

taxonomy: Science dealing with the identification, naming, and classification of organisms.

volcanic winter: Reduction in global temperature caused by volcanic ash and droplets of sulfuric acid obscuring the sun and raising Earth's albedo (increasing the Earth's reflectivity of solar radiation) after a large and particularly explosive type of volcanic eruption.

Bibliography

Arsuaga, Juan Luis, and Andy Klatt. *The Neanderthal's Necklace: In Search of the First Thinkers*. New York: Basic Books, 2004.

Ponders the uniquely human aspects of cooperation and consciousness, finding ways to integrate the archaeological record.

Binford, Lewis R. *In Pursuit of the Past: Decoding the Archaeological Record*. First ed. with a new afterword. Berkeley: University of California Press, 2002.

Reading Binford can be rough for students of anthropology, but this book, based on a series of lectures, may be the most personal introduction to his thinking.

Boaz, Noel Thomas, and Russell L. Ciochon. *Dragon Bone Hill: An Ice-Age Saga of* Homo erectus. Oxford, NY: Oxford University Press, 2004.

A history and interpretation of the Peking Man discovery of *Homo erectus* at Zhoukoudian, China.

Clottes, Jean. *Cave Art*. repr. ed. London: Phaidon Press, 2010.

Beautifully illustrated, large-format book with photos from all the major Upper Paleolithic painted caves in Europe, and a small collection of portable objects and art from other parts of the world.

Cochran, Gregory, and Henry Harpending. *The 10,000 Year Explosion: How Civilization Accelerated Human Evolution*. New York: Basic Books, 2009.

Discusses Neandertal genetics and the recent rapid evolution of human genes from a point of view that is very similar to Professor Hawks's.

Falk, Dean. *Braindance: New Discoveries about Human Origins and Brain Evolution*. New York: Henry Holt, 1992.

A review of Falk's ideas about brain evolution, including the "radiator theory."

Fischman, Josh. "Family Ties: Dmanisi Find." *National Geographic* (April 2005): 16–27.

This illustrated feature article describes the Dmanisi site and discusses the importance of small body size in the skeletons.

Gibbons, Ann. *The First Human: The Race to Discover Our Earliest Ancestors*. New York: Anchor Books, 2008.

A gripping account that follows the major field teams as they find older and older hominins. Published before the announcement of the Ardi skeleton in 2009.

Guthrie, R. Dale. *The Nature of Paleolithic Art*. Chicago: University Of Chicago Press, 2006.

Guthrie interprets cave art from the perspective of an archaeologist specializing in ancient animals, with fresh insights about hunting practices and how children may have been involved in art production.

Hawks, John. *John Hawks Weblog*. Neandertal DNA tag. http://johnhawks.net/weblog/reviews/neandertal_dna. Accessed May 20, 2010.

Professor Hawks keeps up-to-date notes on the latest findings in the DNA of ancient genomes.

Haynes, Gary. *The Early Settlement of North America: The Clovis Era.* Cambridge, UK: Cambridge University Press, 2002.

A more formal introduction to the topic of the first settlers of North America by an expert archaeologist.

Johanson, Donald C., and Blake Edgar. *From Lucy to Language*. New York: Simon and Schuster, 1996.

A readable introduction to human origins, beautifully illustrated with David Brill's photography.

Johanson, Donald C., and Kate Wong. *Lucy's Legacy: The Quest for Human Origins*. New York: Three Rivers Press, 2010.

This very recent retelling of the Lucy story also touches on the early origin of *Homo* from the AL 666-1 specimen.

Leakey, Louis Seymour Bazett. *Adam's Ancestors: The Evolution of Man and His Culture*. 4th ed. New York: Harper and Row, 1960.

Morell's biography about the Leakey family covers the same material, but Louis Leakey has a unique way of putting together the place of his fossils in the story of human evolution.

Leakey, Richard. *The Origin of Humankind* (Science Masters Series). New York: Basic Books, 1996.

Ponders the uniquely human aspects of cooperation and consciousness, finding ways to integrate the archaeological record.

Morell, Virginia. *Ancestral Passions: The Leakey Family and the Quest for Humankind's Beginnings*. New York: Simon and Schuster, 1995.

Combined biography of Louis, Mary, and Richard Leakey and their discoveries up to 1995.

Morwood, M. J., and Penny Van Oosterzee. *A New Human: The Startling Discovery and Strange Story of the "Hobbits" of Flores, Indonesia*. New York: HarperCollins, 2007.

Morwood's account of his discovery and role in finding its importance.

Olson, Steve. *Mapping Human History: Discovering Our Past Through Our Genes*. Boston: Houghton Mifflin Harcourt, 2002.

The best written of many accounts that explain the relationship between genetics, population size, and migrations.

Pinker, Steven. *The Language Instinct: How the Mind Creates Language*. New York: William Morrow, 1994.

A classic that sets out many of the problems in the evolution of language.

Relethford, John. *Reflections of Our Past: How Human History Is Revealed In Our Genes*. Boulder, CO: Westview Press, 2003.

A great book written by an anthropological geneticist. Discusses population bottlenecks, the out of Africa hypothesis, Neandertal genes, more recent historical topics, and includes chapters on the Neolithic of Europe, settlement of the New World, and Polynesia.

Savage-Rumbaugh, E. Sue, and Roger Lewin. *Kanzi: The Ape at the Brink of the Human Mind*. New York: John Wiley and Sons, 1994.

An early biography of the famous bonobo, with a review of scientists' attempts to teach language to nonhuman primates.

Schick, Kathy Diane, and Nicholas Toth. *Making Silent Stones Speak: Human Evolution and the Dawn of Technology*. New York: Simon and Schuster, 1993.

Possibly the best general book on how archaeologists use stone tools to interpret the past.

Schoenemann, P. Thomas. "Evolution of the Size and Functional Areas of the Human Brain." *Annual Review of Anthropology* 35 (2006): 379–406.

A scholarly review that covers the main topics in the size and shape of hominin brains.

Shipman, Pat. *The Man Who Found the Missing Link: Eugene Dubois and His Lifelong Quest to Prove Darwin Right*. Cambridge, MA: Harvard University Press, 2002.

Pat Shipman's biography gives the context behind the discovery of the Trinil *Homo erectus* specimens in Java.

Stringer, Chris. Homo britannicus: *The Incredible Story of Human Life in Britain*. London: Penguin Books, 2007.

This focuses on the habitation of Britain over the last million years but has a rich section on the preneandertal inhabitants of Europe.

Stringer, Chris, and Robin McKie. *African Exodus: The Origins of Modern Humanity*. New York: Henry Holt Paperbacks, 1998.

This is a book by one of the most prominent scientists in the modern human origins debate at its height.

Trinkaus, Erik, and Pat Shipman. *The Neanderthals: Changing the Image of Mankind*. New York: Knopf, 1993.

A great historical sketch of the discovery and understanding of Neandertals in human evolution. Not quite up-to-date anymore, but excellent for the historical perspective.

Walker, Alan, and Pat Shipman. *The Wisdom of the Bones: In Search of Human Origins*. New York: Knopf, 1996.

Walker and Shipman lay out the case for a massive increase in body size with *Homo erectus*, based on the interpretation of the Nariokotome skeleton.

Wolpoff, Milford H. "*Ramapithecus* and Hominid Origins." *Current Anthropology* 23, no. 5 (1982): 501–522.

After *Ramapithecus* was shown not to be a hominin, Wolpoff wrote the scientific epitaph—where did paleoanthropology go wrong, and what does it reveal about the science?

Wolpoff, Milford H., and Rachel Caspari. *Race and Human Evolution*. New York: Simon and Schuster, 1997.

Wolpoff and Caspari, 2 of the most prominent scientists in the modern human origins debate at its height, go deep into the history of the problem, describing the lives and ideas of the major players.

Wynn, T., and W. C. McGrew. "An Ape's View of the Oldowan." *Man* 24, no. 3 (1989): 383–98.

This titular article is very readable and lays out the case that early toolmakers shared most of their behavioral capacities with living chimpanzees.

Zimmer, Carl. *Smithsonian Intimate Guide to Human Origins*. New York: HarperCollins, 2007.

Well illustrated and written by one of today's best science writers.

Notes

Notes

Notes

Notes

Notes

Notes